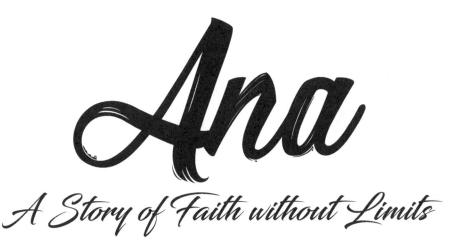

Ana

A Story of Faith without Limits

Voice Of The Light
MINISTRIES

A Story of Faith without Limits

Publisher: Voice Of The Light Ministries / United States of America
Telephone: +1.904.834.2447 - P.O. Box 3418
Category: Autobiography
Design and Edition: Ana Méndez Ferrell
Book Layout: Andrea Jaramillo

© Dr. Ana Méndez Ferrell
www.voiceofthelight.com | www.vozdelaluz.com
1° English Edition 2019, Voice Of The Light Ministries - Ponte Vedra,Florida,32004 / U.S.A

ISBN: 978-1-933163-94-9

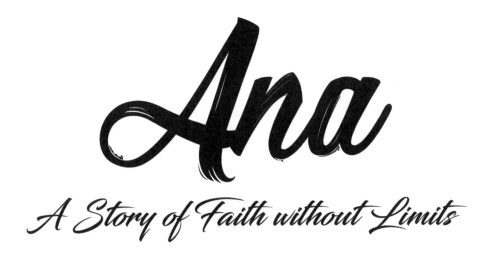

Ana

A Story of Faith without Limits

Dr. Ana Méndez Ferrell

Dedication

I dedicate this book first of all to my Heavenly Father, His Son Jesus Christ and the Holy Spirit, by whom I am what I am. I owe it all to Him.

I also wish to dedicate this book to my husband Emerson Ferrell who has been my greatest support and the love of my life.

To the entire team "Equipo Libertadores" who experienced first-hand this great story of faith and made the challenge possible. And to every intercessor who was also a part of this story.

Index

SECTION 1:

- MY LEGACY -   Page 11

Chapter 1: The Awakening   Page 15

Chapter 2: The Golden Threat   Page. 31
    -Looking Back
    -The Andes and the Amazon Jungle
    -Amazon River
    - Yagua Tribe

Chapter 3:   The Training   Page 59
    -Among Angels
    -The Glove
    -The Popocatépetl Volcano

SECTION 2:

- EVEREST PART 1 -

Chapter 4: Everest, in Sight   Page 83
    -My Motivation

Chapter 5: The First Expedition to Nepal   Page 97
    -How Everything Began
    -Back To Mexico
    -The Challenge
    -The Opposition
    -An Unknown Enemy

Chapter 6: Countdown Begins   Page 125
    -Weakened to the Extreme

Chapter 7: The Moment of Truth   Page 135
    -The Expedition At The Break Of Checkmate

- EVEREST PART 2 -

Chapter 8: En Route   Page 155
    -First Great Battle
    -Great Embarrassment

Chapter 9: The Thengoboche Monastery   Page 171
    -The Sherpa Graveyard
    -Predestination

Chapter 10: The Sacrifice, Door of the Unusual   Page 183
    -The Sacrifice

Chapter 11: General in Charge Takes the Lead   Page 193
    -Visitors in the Death Zone

Chapter 12: A Death Encounter   Page 203
    -The Gentle Voice after the Storm

Chapter 13:
The Dragon's Throat and the Door of the Underworld   Page 213

- EVEREST PART 3-

Chapter 14:
The Heart of the Mountain   Page 225

Chapter 15: Judgment and the Exodus   Page 253

Chapter 16:
The Mortal Incident with Ang Rita -Sherpa   Page 265
    -The Great Surprise
    -Not One Hair Falls Without His Will

Chapter 17: Held Hostage in Katmandú   Page 277
    -An Unknown Weapon

Chapter 18: The Fruit   Page 285

Ana
A Story of Faith without Limits

Section

1

Ana

A Story of Faith without Limits

Section 1

My Legacy

I write this book as a legacy for future generations, so they too might know the power of God as I, myself, have experienced it in my own life.

God is real, and the spiritual world is not a fictional one. Understanding it, knowing its laws and transforming it is the true power Jesus Christ has left us to change a world that is immersed in darkness.

We all have been given a measure of faith as an everlasting key deposited within each one of us, which should we choose to use, will lead us to come to know the true and living God. However, faith does not end there, and embracing it as our greatest treasure allowing it to guide our destiny and challenge our natural mind, will lead us to the most amazing realms and pathways of the supernatural imaginable.

History has always been changed by those willing to embrace an impossible cause with all their heart, and determined to see it through.

In my case, I believe in the Son of God, Jesus Christ, who came into this world to destroy the works of the devil and to transform a world full of darkness into a Kingdom of light and peace.

My goal, and the force that fuels it, is to deliver as many people as possible from this world full of darkness, pain, ignorance and death, even at the expense of my own life. This is a story of a limitless faith that has always believed that the greatest exploits can be achieved in God. In this book, I will share many of my supernatural experiences, which most people, whose minds are used to seeing the material world as their only reality, may struggle to realize the truth behind the unseen reality.

There is an invisible world that governs all things. It is a dimension beyond the matrix of this world, similar to the movie that bears the same name, wherein two realities interconnect, one which is ruled by the slavery of a system that strips man from his eternal nature leaving him blind, and another by those willing to take the red pill[1] and be transformed to overcome the yoke imposed by this so called matrix. These are the ones born of the Spirit of God,

---

1 In the movie, the main character has to take a red pill to enter into the invisible dimension

who have sought the Lord in such a way that He entrusts them with the keys of His kingdom.

These are also the ones who have managed to explore the mysteries of the ages and have been granted access into the glorious dimensions pierced through by some of the greatest men of the Bible such as: the Apostle John, who was taken up to see the realms of heaven described in the book of Revelation, Enoch who walked with God and then simply crossed over the eternal threshold and disappeared, Ezekiel and Elijah whose bodies and spirits were transported into these inaccessible regions to the natural man.

Moreover, these realms are still available for those whom God in His infinite grace chooses to reveal them to.
Therefore, beloved readers open your mind to go beyond the world you currently know, and be transported to places where faith takes on its true strength: where the God of the invisible becomes real.

This is my story or at least part of it, which has transformed me into the woman I am today. There are many incredible experiences and extraordinary battles I will go into in future sagas, however this is the story that started it all. It describes how faith took me to the top of the mountain and turned me into the person I am today.

The Awakening

I had wasted many of my years pursuing empty goals, seeking to overcome the intense pain brought about by the life I had endured. During my first marriage, I had suffered both physical and emotional abuse and lost the custody of my two children. Lack and poverty kept me bound to their unrelenting yoke. My heart was broken time and time again by every manner of betrayal and unfortunate situation.

Seeking a way out, I fell into the clutches of the occult. The crushing pain of not having my children with me, coupled with this dark and brutal trap, led to my destruction, even to the point of attempting suicide by slitting my wrists.

In this darkness, the enemy led me to experience first-hand, unbearable emotional torture that cannot be easily endured. No physical pain can ever compare to the pain found in the soul. My involvement in the occult opened my whole being as a habitation for demonic spirits which constantly lashed at me as they pleased destroying my life and everything that I had.

Day and night, year after year, they never ceased harassing me as they painstakingly sought to control my life by flooding my mind with terrifying lies. I can only liken it to horror movies, continually playing out in my mind, causing me to go over every possible way to end my own life.

I know all too well the meaning of the word darkness: when life is completely void of a single ray of hope; with no escape whatsoever from affliction, sorrow, and solitude. It is like living in an infinite dark prison, with no way out, sleepwalking with a bleeding and shattering heart in my hands. Little by little, less of me was left, and everything I ever loved was stripped away from me.

Once the devil grabs a hold of your pain, he quickly turns it into rage and hatred towards everything else. The spirits of jealousy and self-destruction feed on this anger. I could feel the struggle within me, like ravenous wolves tearing at me on the inside. I use this term because I could literally feel their claws tearing at me.

I came to understand that once a soul reaches its breaking point, it turns numb, entering a type of lethargy wherein nothing is felt for a season of time. It's a moment of artificial peace and death, that is, until the pain returns once again with even greater force.

I had lost all hope, the will to live, and sunken deeper into darkness until I had hit rock bottom.

Perhaps, I would dare to say that I am one of those individuals who have experienced a tiny sample of the horrors of hell while still alive. The devil led me to see the tortured and burnt souls of the lost at the destructive joy of their tormentors.

No words can describe the blackness of that darkness, blacker than the darkest, most inconceivable imagination. I could easily describe on pages without end, the maddening inexistence of all hope, and above all, the terrifying and daunting absence of God.

However, that is not the end of my story, but just the beginning. This book is not about all the circumstances and misfortunes that shred my life into pieces, nor about how to arise out of them, since I have already written several books on this subject before.[2] This volume is about the victories that helped me emerge, and gave meaning to my existence.

This is the story about the power of God in the life of a person who valued every last drop of the blood shed by Jesus for her, and who made up her mind to leave a mark on millions of people by helping them understand how to transform the spiritual atmosphere they live in.

---

2 Regions of Captivity, Iniquity, High Level Warfare. Published by Voice of the Light Ministries. www.voiceofthelight.com

Encountering Jesus and making Him the Lord of my life healed me completely. It changed my perspectives, values, and goals in life. It led me to not only forgive everyone who had ever hurt me but love them, as well. From the very first day of my conversion in that psychiatric ward where my brokenness finally came to an end, my life was literally underwent a one hundred and eighty degree transformation. The change was just as radical as Saul's conversion on the road to Damascus, which ended up turning him into the great Apostle Paul.

It all began on the day that my shattered soul heard the sweet voice of a pastor sharing about the great sacrifice the Son of God had made for me. The hospital room was filled with a powerful presence that frightened me at first. My soul was so filled with hurt and pain that I could not understand exactly what was transpiring before me. My body started to shake, and the room seemed to disappear as an intense, luminous cloud began to fill it. I slowly lifted my head and there, before me, was a dire vision of Jesus nailed to the cross.

His face swollen and disfigured stained by blood and dirt. His eyes almost completely shut due to the beatings he had endured, gazed at me with such love and mercy constraining my heart and whispering to me, "I did all this for you, because I love you."

I began to see my name written on all His wounds. It was not difficult to understand that it was my sins, my offenses, and my awry decisions that were responsible for nailing Him to that cross.

His body was reflected in mine, as a dim yet all-revealing light that allowed me to see into the true condition of my soul. My garments were torn and defiled with the stench of filth. I could see my face through a hideous mirror of the deepest darkness.

> - I thought there was no one more miserable and worthless than me. "Could He really forgive me?" was the question that lingered in my mind after having wounded Him so much."

Broken and weeping inconsolably, I asked for His forgiveness.

I could then see His blood flowing from the cross, cleansing all my sins, my garments, and changing everything within me. It was like a potter breaking a vessel and making it new again.

His presence began to radiate like a wonderful light, full of love and might. I could feel His glory running through my body like a powerful electric current.

Both, the pastor and I, fell to the ground as the glory of God filled the room. We were unable to move for hours. I vaguely remember when he left the room, and it was not until the following day that I was able to see everything with such clarity.

I felt free, like a horrid oppression had lifted off me. I was filled with a vitality I had never experienced before. My mind was extraordinary vivid, and every pain and sickness had completely disappeared from my body.

I stared at myself in the bathroom mirror. For quite some time now, I had seen my face deteriorating in a deep sorrow and depression, sinking me in a pit of pain and despair. Gazing at my lost and somber appearance, with dark rings formed by so many shed tears, had stripped me of all hope of ever being normal again.

However, on that particular day, I saw the reflection of someone totally different in the mirror. My face looked young, and radiant, and all the dark circles were gone. My eyes gleamed like those of a little girl full of peace and innocence. My heart had become a fountain of joy that overflowed with the laughter of thankfulness and hope.

I decided to take a stroll through the hospital's corridors. I would see the sick with great compassion, but I no longer felt like I was one of them. The more I looked at them recalling all the pain I myself had endured, the greater a divine rage formed within me. Noticing all the lies, oppression and pain with which darkness tortures this world became unbearable.

Pain breeds rage caused by deep wounds that are then fueled by the powerlessness of being unable to help our loved ones. However, there is a rage that can lead to our destruction and that of those around us, and there is another rage that comes from God. The latter one is designed to form men and women of war, heroes who are willing to fight for justice, hate evil and lay down their lives to leave a better world behind them. That was the type of rage that burned within me, and which would soon become my purpose and destiny in life.

My training was soon to begin. The first attack came from none other than the Director of Psychiatry overseeing my case in the hospital.

He walked into my room during his morning rounds, expecting to see the same crushed individual he had seen days before. But instead, he now saw someone filled with joy. He was immediately filled with skepticism, and like every good scientist, tried to persuade me that everything I had experienced was only a mental lapse due to my emotional state.

God's strength kept me strong, though, as I heard the most abhorrent diagnoses stemming from the studies he had performed on me. I never gave in, nor did I fall back into that depressive state which the devil arduously fought hard to drag me back into.

With a calm and steady voice, I looked at him and affirmed,

> -"I know I am healed, but I don't expect you to believe me but I know what happened to me was a wonderful miracle from God. Let's just do the following," I added, as I stared at the wild graphics displayed on the encephalogram that was done on me. "I challenge you to run those tests on me again."

-"Ha!" He laughed. "I have seen many cases like this. Mentally ill patients want to grab onto a life board, leading them to engage in these mystical experiences. But all right, I'll carry out a series of tests on you just to show you how severe your situation really is. We will get started this afternoon."

In that moment, I heard the voice of God within me for the first time.

-"Don't look back. My strength and power are with you. Remain steadfast in the truth for I am that Truth."

The voice filled me with such strength and conviction amazing me. No, it was not my imagination, because that wasn't my normal reaction under pressure.

Knowing the Truth, and standing on it, was the foundation of my total freedom; but the real battle lied in remaining steadfast to it, and rejecting every lie that the devil would employ to entangle my mind.

Throughout the following ten days, they locked me in a room for two hours a day with a doctor whose sole mission was to prove to me that my depressive state was incurable.

She performed psychological tests on me that I would never wish on anyone. Every session felt like she would stab at the unbearable and painful places of my heart, albeit not to help and heal me, but just to prove her diagnosis.

She never broke me, but I came out victorious in all of them. However, to be honest, it was quite an intense and unfamiliar battle for me.

Many internal questions and doubts were stirred up within me, and I had to destroy every one of them by embracing God's love, which had now become my truth.

Emerging from this condition with a shattered heart was going to require faith and learning to receive the love and power that comes from God. This was key, since the first thing we lose when faced with intense pain is the ability to receive and believe in love. I had to make this now my focus and the basis for my new life. Above all things, I determined in my heart that everything was possible with God, and that no one would ever stray me from that decision.

On the one hand, I was defeating internal structures, and on the other, I was exercising my faith in the power of God.

After my conversion, Pastor Christian would come to visit me on a regular basis. His second visit followed a harrowing experience with a mental patient who had spent the entire night screaming in excruciating pain. Nobody slept that evening. At dawn, they locked her up in a padded room filled with bloodstained scratches from previous patients. If this didn't work, she would undergo electro-shock treatments. But still even worse was another step that involved disconnecting her brain.

During that horrible night, the rage within me grew even more. Then a thought entered my heart as clear as the light of day: If God had healed me; He could also do the same for everyone else in there. I waited anxiously for Christian3 and as soon as he arrived, I immediately shared what I had heard during those evenings at the hospital. And I suggested the idea of going door to door sharing Jesus and healing every patient.

There was a glimmer in my eyes that reflected my conviction.

-"How could we do this? What do we need to do to heal and deliver them?" I asked.

He looked at me with shock and disbelief, not so much questioning whether it could be done, but because it was I who had come up with the idea.

He then changed his reaction and nodded, as if it was the easiest thing to do.

-"The Bible says that these signs will follow those who believe": "In my name, Jesus said, you will drive out demons; you will speak in new tongues; you will pick up snakes with your hands; and when you drink deadly poison, it will not hurt you at all;

you will place your hands on sick people, and they will get well."**4**

-"Do you believe this?" He asked.

-"Of course I do, let's go!" I exclaimed.

The first door we knocked on was Carmen's room, an older lady who had suffered a stroke and was left paralyzed with minimal mental ability.

I was excited, because I knew that I knew that God would do a miracle. Christian looked at me as if saying, "This is a pretty serious case!" But, his heart was also full of determination.

I told Carmen what Jesus had done for me. After all, she had noticed my condition when I had first arrived, just like the other psychiatric patients.

-"And I know that He can also do the same for you, Carmen" I continued.

She smiled as we led her to ask forgiveness for her sins and receive Jesus Christ into her heart. Then we laid our hands on her head and prayed. Instantly she expressed,

-"Something like liquid is flowing inside of my head. I feel an intense heat." Her voice became clearer as she spoke. She looked at us lively and said,

-"Help me get up!"

Christian and I looked at each other and marveled. Carmen got up and ran through the hospital garden shouting joyfully and glorifying God, and causing a tremendous ruckus since everyone was aware of what her condition was. The doctors and nurses recognized that something supernatural was happening but still held on to their exclusive belief in science. Nonetheless, God began to win them over silently.

Carmen's case opened the doors for us to pray for every patient so they could receive Jesus in their hearts. After ten days, we had delivered over eighty percent of the patients in that hospital through the power of Christ.

However, management, indirectly led by Catholic priests,5 quickly got wind of these events. The hospital, after all, belonged to the Catholic Church, and for them converting to Christ and following the Bible was reason for persecution the likes of the Inquisition, which has never stopped taking place since the times of Martin Luther. So, the priest in charge began to look for a way to kick me out of the hospital.

On the other hand, the director of psychiatry was hearing about everything that transpired every day. He also appreciated how much stronger and secure in the faith I was, so he decided to discharge me from the hospital.

---

5) Hospital Español de la Ciudad de México, pabellón psiquiátrico. 1985

Our final interview was a touching and moving. The arrogant doctor who had once tried to prove how irreparable my condition was, had let his guard down little by little, and was now amazed at the eminent change he was seeing in me.

-"Oh! How I wished I could believe with that same kind of faith that you have," he beamed. "But unfortunately, this career has made me too rational ... but perhaps one day..." he added as he sighed.

Then he asked,
-"Hey, is it alright if I call you right before I have to disconnect a patient? Maybe you can speak with them so we don't have to unplug them."

-"Of course," I replied.

-"I also have a question," I added. -"When I went to pay my hospital bill this morning they only charged me seventy pesos (approximately seven dollars at that time). I know this is incorrect, and I want to leave here knowing that I have paid the right amount in full."

On the inside I was in distress because I knew I did not have a single cent to cover it, but I would rather borrow the money than do something that was not right.

-"That is the correct amount," he affirmed with a
smile. "I spoke with hospital management last night
and we agreed that we would only charge you for the
nurse that tended to you the night you arrived.
I arranged it so that you wouldn't be charged any
more than that. We really didn't do anything for you
other than hold you back. Your God made you whole,
and therefore I cannot charge you."

I was shocked. Not only did God save my soul, healed
my body, and delivered and healed the patients in the
psychiatric ward, but now He even covered my hospital
bill. Wow!

-"Thank you, Doctor. We are going to stay in
touch and I know that one day, you too will believe."

We embraced and said good-bye. He did call me after
that a couple of times to pray for some patients and God
continued glorifying His name in that hospital.

The Golden Thread

Everything that happens in life, how we are born, where we grow up and the circumstances that form us are all part of the building blocks of an internal structure being molded within us.

Every decision we make as we grow up, start to form the construct that makes us who we are today.

Even our mistakes, and the most horrible sins, tragedies, injustices and abuses that we may have committed or may have been a victim of, have a purpose in the fulfillment of our destiny. There is a golden thread in everyone's life that joins events chosen by God to form a complete design, and the greatest privilege that any person can have is to discover it. When we do, we realize that the hand of the

Almighty One was always there surrounding, shaping, sculpting, breaking and re-shaping us until we are finally configured into His divine plan.

Unfortunately, not everyone comes to this understanding. We are only able to decipher the hidden messages and strategic blows of the chisel of God in the light of eternal understanding. It's only in this light that we learn to appreciate how the great sculptor of our life shapes us day in and day out. Once this light shines, we notice the huge chunks of rock that must still be chipped away, and the large amount of useless material that must be removed from us.

In my case, on the one hand, God would form a general for spiritual warfare as a strategic weapon, used in His mighty hand, to undo the works that destroy mankind, oppress him, and pull him away from his Creator. God needed someone willing to overcome every type of fear and confront hell itself to pluck out souls from the devil's grasp.

On the other hand, God also needed to form someone who would understand His Majesty, His Glory and His Infinite Love to establish millions of people in His Kingdom of power and greatness.

He had to mold me in different ways to form within me His compassion, His values and His unwavering perseverance and love, which is the strongest force in the universe.

Looking Back

I wasn't born like most people are, as an individual with my own name and personality. I came into this world as an identical twin. Scientifically speaking, I was the accident of a cell that split in two, and instead of one fertilized egg, we were half and half.

At the time we were born, there was no way of knowing the sex of the fetus. Parents had to wait for the big day we were delivered to get the surprise.

My father was a widower with three sons when he married my mother. Now, faced with a fourth child was a big challenge for him. Although he was a wealthy businessman, he was not very fond about having many children. When he found out we were two girls, he turned sour, instantly rejecting us as well as our mother.

Inside the womb, during our gestation period, my twin sister was always on top of me, yet somehow, I managed to come out first. The constriction caused by so many months in that position caused me to be quite frail, barely weighing in at about 3 pounds at birth. My sister, on the other hand, weighed in at about 4 pounds and was beautiful from the very moment she came into this world.

I, however, was pretty much sentenced to death. The first words out of the doctor's mouth were that I would not

5) Gemelas de un mismo óvulo

survive. So, they placed me in an incubator and fed me with a dropper since I didn't have enough strength to latch on and drink my mother's milk.

I was literally fighting for my life, side by side with God in that incubator. I am a firm believer that all babies come directly from God, thus in that moment, His great design for my life began to take shape.

Once I overcame this first episode in life, my sister and I lost our names and our identity. No one cared about knowing who was who. The easiest thing for everyone was to refer to us as "the twins." They would dress us alike, and the only thing different about us was a red or green bow on our hair. We would only receive one cake and one gift, for the two of us, on our birthday. Amidst smiles, laughs and everyone's amusement, we were basically being shaped into "half-persons."

Although most people would never understand this, since they have never experienced it, this became a heartbreaking issue when we reached adolescence. We each needed our own name and personality. We needed to be rewarded or rebuked for what each one of us did individually, but everyone refused to grant us that opportunity.

When we turned nine, our parents divorced and we stayed with our mother and younger brother. My mother had to find a job, and our grandmother cared for us. The life of abundance our father had provided for us came to an end, and we had to cut back significantly.

On the other hand, when it comes to twins, there is always one who is more dominant and talented than the other and always ends up with all the talents, leaving the less gifted one in the shadows of the stronger one.

In my case, Mercedes my twin was the life of the party with a fun and engaging personality, known for her intelligence. She hardly studied yet got the highest grades. She also had many admirers, whereas I, on the other hand, was both the ugly duckling and had to study very hard to get a good grade. I would work very hard, because just as you might expect, the pressure exerted on me by my sister's success was quite strong. With such a bright and shining beacon standing next to me, who would even give me the time of day,? I had gone from being referred to as "the twins" to "Mercedes two", or in other words, a zero.

At the age of nineteen, right after graduating from high school, Mercedes was chosen to go to Paris as a foreign correspondent for one of the most important newscasts and largest television networks in Latin America -Televisa. It only took one interview for her to dazzle the company's management, and right away, she was sent to live in Europe.

This is when I saw the opportunity to be someone completely different than her. I was determined to be Ana and define who I really was.

A few months before her departure, I had an experience that marked my life. It happened during the month of

June, while studying hard for my final exams in high school. With such a bright and shining beacon standing next to me, who would even give me the time of day,? I had gone from being referred to as "the twins" to "Mercedes two", or in other words, a zero.

"What was it?" I asked myself. It can't be a real star or an airplane since it wasn't moving. Suddenly a powerful ray of light burst from the star and entered into my bedroom. The room was filled with such an indescribable goodness that it caused me to fall to the floor as if dead. I could not lift my head nor move any part of my body. I began to weep uncontrollably. My heart could not contain itself before the indescribable love that engulfed me. A strange mix of emotions turned within me. I felt tiny and unclean, but also the happiest woman in the world at the same time. I could not understand what was happening, but there in the midst of the light was Jesus, bright and shining like the sun in all His majesty. And He said to me in a gentle voice:

"Write!"

I began to clumsily jot down without giving it much thought. I felt like I was in the middle of all the wisdom and knowledge of God. Not only was everything being revealed to me at the same time, but also I was also able to understand it. The feeling was indescribable.

A strong force came out of Him like an intense gust of wind and light that struck my face. I fell weak to the ground, as the vision disappeared before me.

I'm not sure how many hours had gone by, before I gained my composure while still under the effect of His power. I took the piece of paper to see what I had written, since I was still unable to grasp what had just happened.

The paper read,

"I am Jesus Christ, your Lord and I have come to tell you that in due time, I will reveal myself to you because you will be my servant and I will come to you through a man with blue eyes."

From that point on, I fell deeply in love with Jesus and my search for Him never ended until I finally encountered Him eleven years later in that psychiatric hospital. By the way, Christian the pastor had blue eyes.

This encounter activated extraordinary courage and boldness within me. Despite lacking any type of religious training whatsoever, I somehow knew that God existed. He was real, and He was with me.

Mercedes' departure for Paris was like a detonator going off inside of me to do things I had always wanted to do, yet had been unable to because of my age and the rules I was subject to at home.

God had placed an adventurous and conquering spirit within me, defiant to any type of danger. And now was the time for me to launch out and discover who I really was.

The Andes and the Amazon Jungle

My grandmother, whom we grew up with, was originally from Chile and she would always tell us stories about the Andes Mountain Range. After Chile's great Earthquake of 1900, my family decided to immigrate to the United States and the only way to do so was by crossing the Andes by mule into Argentina and then traveling north by ship.

Ever since I was a little girl and would hear her talk about this great mountain odyssey, my heart would beat faster in excitement for I always knew that one day I would do something similar.

The timing was perfect. I had a Chilean friend whose parents became acquainted with my father during their stay in Mexico under General Allende's dictatorship. Following the coup of 1974, they decided to return to their country and invited me to visit them.

This was my opportunity. I patched together some money I had saved with some my mother had given me and headed off to Chile. I had a much bigger plan, though, than just simply visiting my friend.

After spending two weeks with them, I cancelled my return flight and used the refund to embark on my adventure. I traveled by bus, with my friend and her mother, towards Antofagasta in the northern part of Chile, and there we bid farewell.

Since I didn't have much money, I found the cheapest way to cross the Andes that meant crossing from Tacna, the Peruvian border, all the way to Puno. My only option was an old, run down bus with half of the windows missing and a door that had to be shut with a rope. I boarded the bus to find a seat and before I realized it, I was the only person on the bus who spoke Spanish. The rest of the people were of indigenous origin and only spoke the Quechua dialect.

I sat next to one of them and they were astonished when they saw me, albeit not so much by my race, but by my choice of garments. I was wearing jeans and a light sweater, whereas they all looked like Eskimos, covered from head to toe in ponchos and wool hats. Being young and ignorant, it never crossed my mind that temperatures would dip to 20° below zero once you crossed the Andes, and since I had never told anyone about my crazy adventure, no one was able to warn me about this.

Our trip started around six in the evening, with chickens tied to luggage and swoops of dust that blew in through the windows. We started by driving up the mountain range. The road was part paved and part dirt, and the bus had faulty suspension. We could feel every bump and stone on the road. The temperature had quickly dropped by sundown, and the cold wind blew in from everywhere. I quickly started to feel the frigid temperatures but I didn't have anything to cover myself with. The passenger next to me felt sorry for me and gave me a piece of cloth to place over my head. I was curled up in a ball trying to warm myself up with my own body, while my arms and legs started going numb.

Around five in the morning, the bus broke down and we were stranded in the middle of the mountains, with strong gusts of wind sweeping through the hills.

A good amount of time went by before a freight truck stopped and told us to climb in the back like cattle. I could not move my legs, which were already stiff by now, because of the cold. Two men had to carry me out and place me in a corner on the truck bed. Everyone spoke in Quechuan and no one could explain anything to me. We headed towards Puno. The temperature kept on getting colder and colder, and my vital signs began to take a turn for the worse. I couldn't speak, my jaw was locked, and all I could feel was a lone teardrop on my cheek. I felt like my life was coming to an end.

Upon seeing my condition, one of the men began to pound on the cabin window. I was practically unconscious when they placed me inside on top of the passengers, who had agreed to travel the rest of the way like this, to save my life.

I was very close to God in those moments, believing in Him and facing death due to my own folly. But as I mentioned before, even our own foolishness is part of that golden thread and chisel in God's hands. Coming out alive from that deadly circumstance, forged in me a brave and victorious heart. No doubt, that experience would leave me with something very powerful that God would later use to take me to the highest mountains on the planet.

Upon arriving in Puno, by the shores of Lake Titicaca, I began to recover until I felt strong enough to continue on my audacious trip.

Amazon River

I arrived at Iquitos, a city by the Amazon River in Peru. According to my research, primitive boats sailed from there that could drop me off by the edge of the river in the Amazon rainforest. I would then have to cross-rugged terrain until I reach one of the Pygmies villages known as "Yaguas".

There are certain things that make no sense to our human logic, but they are still the foundations of our faith, which go on to become diving boards of our mighty exploits.
What was leading me to one of the most inhospitable regions of the Earth? It was an insatiable thirst for adventure. I needed to find myself. I wanted to be "me"; stripping away every label the world had always placed on me.

Where did King David get the boldness and skill to confront a lion and a bear while he was still a child and a shepherd boy? It is the innate knowledge of God that lives and breathes inside the heart of man, which some are able to hear at an early age. It is confidence; wisdom and supernatural intuition where eternity manifests and makes you feel invincible, immortal, and triumphant over any challenge. This is where you take steps that appear maddening to all human reasoning and survival. It is also thanks to this attitude mankind has conquered, some of the most dangerous places on the planet and in the universe.

Faith breeds and grows inside of us. It does not come from other people's influence. It is God in us, connecting us with everything He is, and that He has designed for us.

That was what drove me to such madness: crossing the Amazon rainforest on my own!

Purity and innocence make us brave, like a small child unafraid of anything. This is how I entered into the perverse city of Iquitos, located by the edge of the enormous Amazon River.

Walking through the city, trying to find a low cost hostel to stay in was like walking through the streets of Sodom and Gomorrah. I finally found a place where I paid one dollar to stay the night. I tried to lock and secure the door with everything I could find. I was unable to sleep that first night, crying out to God for His divine protection. I just wanted the night to pass swiftly by, for I could tell by the noises I heard, that I was probably in the worse hotel in town.

Early the next morning I walked towards the port. I was able to store my luggage in the hotel as I set off with a small backpack, filled with only the most basic items for survival.

The small dock was surrounded by an outdoor market. I was horrified to see skinless monkeys cut up every which way like children hanging from wires in a chicken slaughter house. There were also shrunken human heads their mouths sewn shut. They were probably enchantments, not real, eventhough some of them might have been. They claimed it was how they worked the heads of those who were eaten by cannibals in the jungle.

This was the first blow to my conscience and the first intimidating voice that struck my heart. Visible reality is the worst enemy of faith, locking you up in a box filled with antagonizing voices that scream out the loudest dangers and remind you of your weakness and frailty in life. It becomes a monster that seeks to cripple you and make you feel helpless, as it wields its sword of fear with skillful distress. And if your faith does not tear it apart, it is sure to butcher your greatest exploits.

But the heart of a pioneer and a conqueror is greater than reason, just like that of a child's. The heart grows on the inside and begins to carve the most adverse circumstances, making them smaller and conquerable.

No one has ever accomplished anything extraordinary by relying on his or her reasoning or the opinion of the status quo.

So, I forced my heart to crush the head of that antagonizing voice of reality and figure out how to get to the village of the Yaguas. I had a small map I had found in a booklet, which helped me locate one of the boats that would take me to one of the locations by the riverbank, and from there I would have to journey by foot into the jungle.

A storm arose after four hours sailing. The rustic barge, covered with a piece of sheet metal and filled with natives, banana stalks, skinless monkeys and chickens, struggled to stay afloat. Waves came into the boat, for more than an hour as we relentlessly removed the water. One could feel tensión and fear en everybody's eyes as the riverbank disapeared behind the torrential rain. When finaly everything returned to calm, the boatman steered towards the side and told me I had arrived at my destination.

I was surprised to find absolutely nothing there, except for a thick, impenetrable jungle. I stepped off the boat, in that obscure location, and watched as my last contact with the familiar slowly floated away.

The storm had turned the dirt ground into a swampy marsh. There was absolutely no sign of civilization, but only the river, the jungle and me. Once again, my ignorance was producing more excruciating consequences. I did not have a machete, a lantern, food nor water. I found myself in the exact, same situation as someone who was shipwrecked. There was no point in complaining about my blunder, so I looked for a tree trunk to sit on and think about what I was going to do next.

It was about five in the afternoon and nightfall was slowly closing in. After an hour, I saw at a distance, what appeared to be the figure of a man walking towards me. My heart began to beat with hope, but also adrenaline from what might also be a very eminent danger. I began to pray the only way I knew how, reciting "the Lord's Prayer" over and over again.

I began to relax when I saw that he was an elderly man who seemed nice, and even though he had a machete tied to his bag, he looked peaceful and trustworthy.

He was shocked to see a young, light skinned woman who appeared more urban than rural, alone in that site. As He approached me, I smiled and greeted him. I was so elated to find out he spoke Spanish, my mother language.

-"What are you doing here?" he asked. "This place is very dangerous,"

-"I know. I need to get to this village and I don't know how to get there," I replied as I showed him the map. "Will you please help me?" I asked. "I can't spend the night here."

Boat in which we passed the storm

I pulled out a few dollars I had with me and offered them to him.

The man must have felt quite sorry for me and agreed to take me across the jungle. We were about two hours away, but the quagmire caused by the rain had made it very difficult to walk at a good pace. In fact, there was spots where we were up to our knees in mud.

The jungle noises began to get louder as nightfall approached. There were gigantic toads, the size of cantaloupes that came at us from all sides as well as spiders. Insects, birds, and monkeys communicated with each other in the most unbelievable songs, sounds, beeps, and whistles. Everything was intense and alive, as they conversed in every possible exotic wildlife language.

All we had was the waning light from a lantern that was quickly running out of battery. So, the man suggested that we save some energy. But the only way to do this was to quickly light the way before us, turn off the lamp and recall the path ahead by memory to keep on walking.

At a certain point, we had to walk over a tree trunk, but as we stepped on it, it moved and scurried into the bush. As it turns out, it was a thick snake that we couldn't make out because of the darkness. I felt like my heart stop, but the confidence my guide showed as he fearlessly made his way through the brush, filled me with boldness.

We had walked about four hours non-stop, when we began to see the village's straw rooftops in a wide clearing in the jungle, faintly lit by moonlight.

My happiness however, quickly turned to doubt when the man cautioned, "This is as far as I will go. I'm not going in there! Good luck!" He turned around, and without saying another word, disappeared into the bush.

Why would he not want to go in? I asked myself. Are they cannibals? Would this be the final blow to my ignorance and audacity? What do I do now? Everyone was asleep, and I would not dare knock on a single door.

Then suddenly, a flash of childish enlightenment hit me, a strategy that could save me from any possible peril. I stood in the middle of the village, as the moon shone, and began to sing what I thought sounded like an angelic song. In my teenage innocence, I decided to play the role of an angel or an extraterrestrial being that had come to their village to help them.

Shortly after singing my improvised melody, the villagers started coming out with lit torches in their hands. They were very small, with the tallest one about my chest level. They quickly surrounded me and were aghast by my presence. But to be honest, everyone was in a state of shock, as we gazed at each other under the moonlight.

I remained stoic, unaffected, and focused on my singing as if there was nothing else more important in life to me.

As they perused me from a distance, the witch doctor and the chief of the tribe appeared, both dressed in their corresponding attire and paraphernalia representative of their roles. The witch doctor was the first to approach me and touch my arm to make sure I was flesh and bone. I looked at him with absolute peace, confident in my made-up role. The witch doctor signaled to the others and uttered something in an incomprehensible dialect. The villagers bowed to him and moved back. Then the chief directed me to follow him, allowing me to spend the night in his presidential cabin so to speak. Afterwards, he left along with the witch doctor.

The cabin had no windows but just a few average-height walls and a large opening with a view of the jungle , which turned out to be the bedroom. The cot was made out of woven hay and it had a mosquito net, which I truly appreciated. I fell asleep deeply exhausted, but grateful to God for His favor upon me.

The following morning, as soon as the sun came up, the jungle looked completely different. I was still fast asleep when I started to feel a small hand touching my face in an odd way. I woke up startled, thinking that I would run into one of the Pygmies in the bedroom, but as I opened my eyes, a cute monkey who had come to greet me, let out a shout, leaping in mid- air. I couldn't help but laugh uncontrollably.

The most beautiful landscape of sharp greens and other wonderful colors were unveiled before me. There were two macaw parrots on the bedroom rail that looked like two guardians in fine clothing highlighting the beauty of the jungle. One of the tributaries of the Amazon River flowed by the village. The sound of water could be heard harmonizing a majestic melody of life, coupled with birds and every other type of singing animal.

Yagua Tribe

While I took in the beautiful scenery and meditated on everything that had transpired in the last 36 hours, someone knocked on the door and opened it.

They were three women from the village. They had come to bring me a hay-woven skirt , a breastplate and a crest made of feathers. They cheerfully laid them on my bed and gestured for me to put them on. I did so, and then they took some fruit with a deep red color on the inside and painted stripes on my face as was customary in the tribe. Later, I understood that those were tribal garments of great honor, just like the red marks on my face.

The Pygmies adopted me as one of their own. I stayed in the village for about fifteen days, wherein I learned basic aspects of their dialect, and I helped them in many ways.

Although I was a woman, they did not leave me to help with domestic chores but invited me to go out hunting with the men. They were skilled blowpipe hunters, and I helped them assemble the darts with fish bone and snake venom.

When we would go out looking for animals to feed the tribe, they seemed enthusiastic, letting me know that my presence among them had brought great blessing on their hunting.

We would eat whatever we found, everything from monkeys, serpents, iguanas to diverse fruits. One night, we went looking for an alligator. Six of us launched out in two small boats and navigated down one of the streams in the thick jungle.

Stream where we hunted for alligators

There were moments when vegetation enclosed the river, forming large tunnels where we had to lay on our backs, on the boat, and pull ourselves forward by tugging on the branches over our heads. The tunnels, though, were full of insects and luminous spiders, and we only had the flicker of a small lantern to light the way.

Once we had crossed the branched tunnels, I shined the light towards the edge of the river, in search of an alligator's bright eyes. One of the villagers steered the boat, while the other stood ready to attack with his spear. All of a sudden, we saw one. It paused, dazed for just a moment, and before it was able to dive back underwater, the hunter lunged at it with all his strength driving his spear right through it. And that is when the real battle began. The animal twisted and jerked violently with the spear still in it, as the hunter hauled him on the boat to finish the kill, aided by one of his peers. The boat tumbled as the gator desperately fought to survive. Finally, between the two of them, they managed to slay it. It was a very large beast taking up almost the entire boat. Everyone celebrated the conquest and returned to the village weary but happy at the same time.

When it came time for me to leave, they did not want me to go and would have done just about anything for me to stay. So, I went back to the original role I portrayed at the beginning, explaining to them with signs and drawings on the ground that I would disappear that night.

I was already familiar with the jungle, so I thought I could make my way back to the Amazon River if I followed one of the tributaries. So, I waited for the first light of dawn to start my journey. This time, I was completely alone without a single weapon or machete. But the one thing I did have was an absolute confidence that my Heavenly Father would take care of me. Although I didn't really know God that well, save for the experience I had had in my room years back, I could feel His hand protecting me every step of the way.

The further I moved away from the village, the more defenseless, and vulnerable I felt. There were moments when I could feel fear try to stifle my heart as I sensed the gaze of an animal following me.

I did not know where it was, but I could feel its presence stalking me. Every sound of a twig breaking in the near distance would stop me in my tracks. Thousands of hidden eyes stared at me through the thick bush, but I could not see them. I stepped up the pace without ever resting, trying to stay as close as I could to the edge of the river, although at times the vegetation was so thick, all I could was follow its sound.

I had to cross the narrow river, knowing that it was plagued with piranhas. I had seen them many times when I bathed with the women in a stream near the village. The difference then was that we would throw in a piece of meat or animal waste first, to keep them busy while we were in the water, but this time I didn't have anything with me. In addition, I was going to have to risk it and jump into the current to elude the predator that was following me. There was no other alternative.

Furthermore, because of the dense vegetation, I had to cross it several times and it was not easy. Every time I felt something brush against my body, whether it was fish, algae or a branch, my mind would play out horrific imaginations.

It was about noon when I finally made it to the Amazon River. The vast bend, lit by the sun, sparkled in the foliage as it opened up wider. When I saw it, I couldn't help but cry tears of joy and gratitude. Although I was alone, just like when I had first arrived, I was certainly not the same person. I was not just another teenager with a thrill for adventure, but I was someone who had overcome and who could conquer my dreams. I was someone who believed that the impossible is only found in minds that dare to break their limits.

There, standing by the edge of that river, was "Ana" holding the crest of feathers she had decided to keep as a trophy. The history of being "Mercedes two" was dissolving and the person that I was began to emerge. I was born to conquer. But conquer what? I did not know yet, but my heart told me that it was something big.

I would never again be a simple shadow, void of any identity. Ana now existed, and a new world would soon begin to unveil before her.

With all this in mind, I waited for hours until I saw a boat in the distance heading towards Iquitos. I waved at it to pick me up. It slowly made its way towards me and took me back to civilization.

That experience was followed by eleven years where I was molded in the flames of pain. What followed is what the story in this book is about.

Gold, diamonds and the sharpest of swords are forged in fire, under intense pressure and hammer blows. And then they must be extracted from those ovens, those mines and those anvils to reveal their true value.

What we must understand is that God does not abandon us in the midst of suffering, but His hand molds us, fashions us and bears that pain and agony together with us, until the day He appears before us as the glorious door to our salvation.

There is no such thing as time wasted. Everything has a reason and we can see it when we choose to forgive others and love God above everything else. Unfortunately, there are many people who choose bitterness and resentment, closing themselves off. This leaves them blind and bound by their own misfortunes. However, for those who have eyes to see and ears to hear, all things work together for good.

Mi Familia

Mercedes (my twin) and I (1957)

Ana & Mercedes (1997)

My brother Ricardo, my Mother Mercedes Azcarate and
my Father Mauricio Mendez Meardi

My children Ana & Pedro Louceiro and Jordan Ferrell

Emerson and Ana Ferrell

The Training

Threshold of My Faith

Since my conversion at the psychiatric hospital, I knew that my life was destined to serve Christ. I passionately read my Bible. I was amazed to read about the lives of fearless men and women who gave themselves to truly come to know God. As I read about the people of God, used to write the most extraordinary story ever told, my imagination would run wild into places unheard.

Men like Enoch, Elijah and Philip, who were taken up to inconceivable places in the heavenly realms, transported supernaturally in spirit and body from one place to another. Ezekiel, Daniel, Paul and John were all taken to dimensions outside of the reality of this Earth to see and understand things that do not belong to this world. Deborah and Barak who saw the armies of stars combatting in their favor.

It was exciting to read about angels who appeared in so many different ways to help others, bring them messages, and fight their battles. Reading about men like Joshua, whose prayer brought the rotation of the Earth to a stop, or Moses who opened the Red Sea and delivered millions of people from slavery.

This was not a fantasy, but it was God Himself opening an eternal dimension that transforms and restructures the natural world. This is the invisible dimension Christ granted us access so that we might bring them under His justice.

What other story in all mankind can compare to the story of the Israelites?

Each page amazed me, until one day I came across a word that Jesus spoke, and it literally changed my entire existence.

Assuredly, I say to you, among those born of women there has not risen one greater than John the Baptist; but he who is least in the kingdom of heaven is greater than he.
Matthew 11:11

I read it over and over: He who is least in the kingdom of heaven is greater than he!

Jesus said this for anyone who was willing to believe it, and that was me. He had brought His Kingdom to Earth and avowed that the violent could take it by force.

That meant the Bible would no longer be a historical book for me, but it would become the reality of a marvelous universe filled with supernatural events which God had prepared for me to experience. In that moment, I chose to believe that I too could obtain everything those great men and women of the Bible believed for and experienced in their lives.

Very early in my Christian walk, God allowed me to start a church and pastor it. At the same time, I was also coordinating a large international ministry called World Evangelism led by Dr. Morris Cerullo, whom together with his team, were a great inspiration for my spiritual life and vital instruments in my training.

I learned extraordinary levels of faith from this man. I also experienced persecutions by his side, to the point of death, for he was always willing to give his life for Jesus' sake.

That was his legacy in my life, to love God unto death and to love the lost at whatever the cost. I experienced levels of the supernatural power of God alongside him that very few are ever able to.

Among Angels

On one occasion, the catholic bishop of the Nezahualcóyotl Township in Mexico City, hired two-thousand men from the most dangerous gangs of the criminal underworld to come against us in a miracle crusade. He had threatened the mayor telling him that unless he canceled the event, there would be bloodshed on the main square.

We received a phone call from the local government warning us about the threat, but Dr. Cerullo assured us,

> -"We will not cancel the event, but we will see the mighty delivering hand of the Lord in our favor. Whoever chooses not to participate, let him leave now!" No one left. So, we headed over there, ready for the worst, but at the same time praying for God's divine protection.

People started to arrive many hours before the event. It was about five in the afternoon and about five-hundred people had gathered. Most of them were women and children and some paralytics in wheelchairs.

Two hours before the event was scheduled to start, a large convoy of gangs and assassins surrounded us with clubs, spiked weapons and heavy chains, trying to intimidate us, and yelling and ordering us to leave the square. We seemed puny compared to the vast amount of men that encircled us.

Then suddenly, their tone changed as they started to scream in fear.

> -"Let's get out of here! They'll finish us! They never told us there would be so many of them armed to the teeth!" They ran terrified, boarded their buses and left.

God had opened their spiritual eyes to see the enormous army of angels He had sent to defend us.

That evening we witnessed the most extraordinary signs, healings and miracles we had ever seen before in our life.

The Glove

On another occasion, Dr. Rony Chaves arrived in Mexico as part of Dr. Cerullo's apostolic team.

Dr. Rony Chaves

Dr. Rony, along with a group of prophets, had suffered a terrible defeat; a couple of years back, trying to organize an evangelistic event in Mexico City. As they asked themselves what had gone wrong, the Lord gave them a vision. They saw a dreadful ancient castle that operated from the downtown area in the historical district.

In it, there was a dark principality with the likeness of a winged dragon that ruled the city and controlled high-ranking demons throughout Latin-America.

Rony shared this vision during a conference, and suddenly, he took out a glove like the ones used in ancient duels, daring those in attendance, saying:

> - "For way too long, the devil has been slapping the Church in Mexico...Is there anyone here willing to face up to him and dethrone him?"

Without saying another word, he threw the glove on the ground and issued the challenge.

He had barely finished uttering the phrase; when I leapt out of my chair and ran down to grab the glove.

Deep inside, I did not know what it meant, but the divine rage I felt towards satan strengthened and emboldened me to do whatever had to be done. When I got home, I prayed and humbled myself before the Lord.

> -"Here I am. Send me. Teach me how to do this Lord." I cried

And this is how the story of the most powerful training God has ever submitted me to, unfolded.

During the nineties, God taught me to stand up and valiantly challenge darkness in my nation of Mexico. There were many years of great battles, tearing apart demonic structures, which had prevented the gospel from being preached in my country. The cultures and covenants by which nations are formed become the foundation of the spiritual structure that governs them.

Mexico, whose name means "The moon's navel", was consecrated to the devil under the name of Huitzilopochtli. He bestowed the nation to himself by sacrificing the heart of a warlock. The configuration of the entire Mexican idiosyncrasy revolved around the occult, superstition, idolatry, bloodshed, and corruption. Dismantling it would take years and require masterful strategies, which the Holy Spirit would reveal to us.

God has used men and women, who in their time, understood that through the power of God, history could be changed. This was the case for Rees Howels, an English intercessor, who along with a small team of intercessors managed to disrupt the Third Reich and defeat Hitler, through the power of the Holy Spirit.

There is also the case of Hudson Taylor, who understood the power of prayer, opening the doors to China so the gospel could be preached.

Prayer gets God involved in history to change its course. This is what I had learned and what caused my blood to boil with the fire of God.

My intention, at this point, is not to share the history of all these amazing intercessory initiatives, which will no doubt be a part of a future book, but rather to lay a foundation of the spiritual authority God had developed in me for the great challenge that lied ahead.

The Popocatépetl Volcano

It was the beginning of 1995, and I was returning home from a trip to Peru, the plane flew over the Popocatepetl Volcano in Mexico. We had learned and understood the importance that mountains had in the spiritual realm by listening to Rony's teachings and conducting our own research. As I peered out the window and looked at the volcano, I heard the voice of God say:

-"It is time to conquer it."

This was a true diabolic throne in my country. The Popocatepetl and Iztlacihuatl volcanoes rose directly above the valley of Mexico, and their backsides cover the city of Puebla. They are both revered as national icons that represent the Aztec culture.

Popocatepetl and Iztaccihuatl Volcanoes

Legend has it that both volcanoes were lovers. An Aztec prince, and his beloved, who had been put to sleep by a spell.

Aztecs, and warlocks made of both volcanoes altars for their sacrifices. Each year the candlestick of their goddess Tonatzin, -under the deceitful guise of the virgin of Guadalupe- is lit by the fire brought down from its crater, known as the "devil's spine."

Men were secretly decapitated on its slopes to weaken the male's leadership roles and raise up a matriarchal system over the nation.

When I received this instruction from God, the volcano was active. We contacted the governor of Puebla and asked for his support since the whole area was restricted to the public by police due to the dangerous steam and ash fumaroles emerging from the crater.

The governor, fearing the potential destruction of his city, decided to deny our official request to climb the volcano, but agreed to not keep us from doing so, and if we were to go, it was at our own risk. Despite his negativity, there was a part of him that believed that somehow God could use this group of foolhardy individuals. Moreover, He assigned us a volcanologist to keep us informed of the volcano's activity on a daily basis.

The Popocatepetl volcano was shaking approximately eighteen times a day, at about 7 degrees on the Richter scale. Scorching acid and poisonous gases constantly gushed out from cracks that opened up on the ground.

No one in our group of intercessors knew a thing about mountain climbing. We were just a simple group of church people, seeking to fulfill this endeavor, without the proper physical conditioning.

Despite the terrible and threatening circumstances brought on every day by the volcano, God's voice kept getting stronger, insisting that now was the time to climb. This was the first battle that Rony Chaves and I fought together, and it resulted in a beautiful friendship. Although we were both the same age, I recognized him as my spiritual authority, at that point in time.

He was very thin, he has a masculine appearance with a thick mustache, had great courage and spoke with outstanding authority which intimidated many, but not me. I saw his fatherly side and his intense love for lost souls. He would always dare to say and do what no one else would, and that was my attraction for working with him.

This is also where I came to know the unbelievable grit of Liliana Torres6, who later went on to become one of my right-hand persons in spiritual battles, as well as my best friend.

Liliana was a beautiful woman inside and out, and despite her stunning beauty; her heart was even more amazing. She was determined to fight to the death for her nation of Colombia, as well as the other nations of the Earth, no matter the cost.

Both would play crucial roles in the challenge to come, together with my other disciples, Veronica Cabrera and Lorenzo her brother, whom we called Lencho.

They were both young, nineteen and twenty respectively, and I had rescued them from the bowels of misery in the city of Mexico, teaching them and providing a better life for them.

The Ascent

The ascent of the Popocatepetl Volcano was a turning point in our lives. We started our ascent on May 22nd at four in the morning. We had hiked quite a bit, when we came across a herd of forty black bulls that stood in our way. Where did they come from? What were they doing on an active volcano fifteen thousand feet high? This was definitely not normal. It had to be an army of shamans that had come against us.

Witches and warlocks who guard volcanoes are shape shifters and can change their form at will into animals, which is exactly what was happening before us.

Rony and I took the lead and rebuked them in the name of Jesus Christ, commanding them to leave. Little by little, they began to turn around and disappear into the rocks of the steep slope while the first rays of dawn began to shine off the enormous and challenging mountain.

We were close to fifteen thousand feet high and had just demolished a horrendous altar full of fetishes, when the whole mountain started to rumble with an earthquake of at least seven degrees on the Richter scale. The earth shook beneath our feet, as the furious roaring lava sought to oust us from its loins like an angry beast. We held on by digging our ice axes deep in the dirt, as rocks and ashes came rolling down from the top at over hundred and fifty miles an hour.

6) Today she changed her name to Oriana Torres

The wind started to blow strongly, and we feared that we would be whisked away by the strong gusts. While at the top of the peak, the flaming smoke heaved full strength. Despite the severe winds, we managed to climb at great speed as if transported supernaturally by a chariot of fire. Rony went up one way with one team and I took another route with the rest of the climbers. There were trails where we literally disappeared at one level and reappeared at a higher one in the mountain. We didn't feel it in our bodies, but those who were watching us ascend from the Tlamacas ridge below gave us the testimony on how they saw this happening.

That is when the spiritual realm became visible to the eyes of the more than four hundred warriors who took part in the venture. There were about a dozen team members climbing, while the rest remained at the foot of the mountain.

As I mentioned at the beginning of the book: the reality of the invisible world, which was seen or pierced through by the great men and women of the Bible, cannot be understood with the natural mind, but only our spirit can comprehend those dimensions where the Kingdom of God and of darkness manifest. However, to see it, one must first overcome the matrix of this world.

Were it not for so many witnesses, what I am about to share would have all seemed like make believe.

All along the width of the crater, the image of a dragon

began to form out of thin strands of clouds. Moreover, the figures of a woman in the likeness of the goddess Tonatzin also began to take form in its belly. However, it wasn't a cloud because it remained still, never losing its shape throughout twenty minutes of hurricane-forced winds that were bending the fumarole smoke stacks horizontally. We began to pray against that undeniable power of darkness that ruled from that location known as "the devil's spine" and which was now manifesting before our very eyes.

We were still questioning whether it wasn't our imagination trying to make out a shape out of the thin streaks of steam and smoke, but when we rebuked it in the name of Jesus Christ, it turned its head before the eyes of hundreds of spectators, and stared directly at us. And out of its mouth gushed a whitish smoke that tried to engulf us.

> In that moment, I cried out with all my strength, -"We have defeated you by the blood of Jesus Christ, by the word of our testimony, and by laying down our lives even unto death!"

Rony and his team had already made Summit. God had instructed them as a prophetic act against the devil's spine to stick a knife, as a symbolic sword into the crater. The temperature of the ground increased, and flames of fire and brimstone emerge from beneath their feet. They decided to head back down since the danger was imminent.

Not only was seeing this stunning manifestation shocking, in the midst of roars emanating from the flaming lava, but it also coincided with the covenant made on the volcano with the Mixcohatl god, whose name means cloud serpent or cloud dragon. This was precisely what we were seeing before us.

The battle intensified, with six winged beasts materializing in the shape of black clouds rising from the ground and rapidly coming against us.

The demonic oppression and lack of oxygen were suffocating us. We fought with all the authority and power of Jesus Christ, prophesying the Word of God and stretching our hands towards them so the power of God would shred them to pieces. We were declaring in faith bright beams of light coming forth out of us.

Instantly, the Spirit of God warned us about a counterattack that was being unleashed on the neighboring Iztacihuatl volcano, which is also known also as the Dormant Woman.

Feeling the dragon's defeat at her beloved Popocatepetl's crater, she arose to defend him. Out of her white, snowy gown like a bride lying on her stony bedstead, an army of black shadowy figures swiftly made their way towards us. They took the form of humanoids. And though the clouds around them quickly scattered, these shady silhouettes remained unfazed, slowly making their way towards us like a fearless army.

We prayed and raised an invisible wall between the two volcanoes, prophesying that the fire of God would consume them and decreeing that flashes of lightning would shoot forth out of our hands.

An intense heat from heaven suddenly came down melting Iztacihuatl's eternal snow in under ten minutes. Never, had this volcano been seen without it, bare and naked.

Once the battle was over, the intercessors at the ridge between both volcanoes and those at the foot of the mountain, told us how they literally saw rays of light coming out of Popocatepetl towards Iztacihuatl. They told us how these rays struck the "Dormant Woman" melting her white, snowy layers for which she had always been reveled and admired.

We were the first to be surprised. Our minds and our perception were being molded to understand manifestations that we had never seen or heard before.

As we climbed down, a layer of snow that had remained on the side of the volcano where we had been also melted, forming two tumultuous rivers of water and rock, which were not only dangerous but also difficult to avoid. Only God's hand helped us to cross over to the other side.

Once the two teams had regrouped and descended, both Rony and I heard the voice of God that said,

> -"This is just the beginning, I am preparing you for an even greater battle. You shall climb Mt. Everest."

When we reached the bottom, I shared with Rony what I had heard, still stunned by it, and to be honest, also quite skeptical about it as well.

-"I heard the same thing," he gasped.

We both looked at each other puzzled, but how could this be so?

We bid each other farewell, but the voice continued to resonate within me, keeping me up at night for days on end, and filling me with both excitement and distress at the same time. Would I really carry out such an exploit?

The battle in the volcano opened up the heavens over Mexico City and the neighbor city of Puebla. People were coming to Christ by the thousands. One could breath an atmosphere of freedom, and every one who participated grew in faith and power to do great things for God.

In less than a year we held an evangelistic initiative that we called "Operation Jonah" in the city of Puebla. During three weeks we brought the Gospel to nearly three million people, calling them to repent and to turn to God, hundreds of thousands listened and gave their lives to the Lord. In this city that was totally controlled by idolatry and closed to the Gospel, the government gave us permission to preach and provided the sound equipment. The secular radio stations allowed us to preach every day. Most of the churches helped us go door to door. The secular newspapers gave us space to spread the word of repentance to the city. After that the whole city was transformed. Puebla is one of the most developed and prosperous cities in Mexico.

Over a year went by with God building us up in wisdom and knowledge concerning territorial spiritual warfare. For Rony and I it was wonderful to run into each other and exchange the revelations and victories that God had granted us.

The fire of that incredible calling God had placed in both of us continued to grow, and time itself would mark its fulfillment.

Our Route of Ascent

Our Route of Ascent on May 22 nd , 1995

Section

2

Everest

Part 1

Everest, in Sight

During the nineties, I was a part of the "World Intercessory and Spiritual Warfare Network of 2,000 AD," led by Dr. C. Peter Wagner. I coordinated the spiritual battalions in Mexico.

There were approximately 140 nations involved worldwide, with over seventy million intercessors.

The main focus of this worldwide intercessory movement was what is commonly known as the 10/40 window – a geographical zone located between 10 degrees north and 40 degrees north latitude. It was also the least evangelized region in the world. Thousands of leaders, pastors and prayer and evangelism organizations had joined in this great effort.

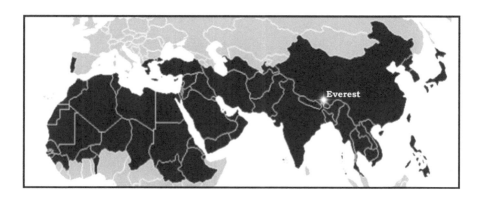

For centuries, missionaries from all over the world had tried to take the gospel into this dark region of the Earth with little to

That is when God showed me a vision through dreams. I could clearly see a structure, like a castle made of ice, on Mount Everest. It was one of the devil's main strongholds on the Earth, filled with many rooms that functioned as a headquarters from where he controlled the nations. There were spiritual highways that connected it to England, India, Lhasa in Tibet and Mexico.

I could hear God's divine voice persisting saying, -"You will never conquer the 10/40 window if you do not first tear down the throne of darkness that is upon Mount Everest."

7) Mark 3: 27

One of the spiritual principles for the deliverance of cities is something that Jesus says concerning being able to enter the house of a strong man and plunder his goods without first binding him up. 7 Only then will you be able to pillage his house. However, in this case, this particular house was located in the highest regions of the planet.

The original name of the mountain in the Nepalese language is Sagarmatha, which means, "The mother goddess of all the universe," and it is located on the border between Tibet and Nepal right in the middle of the Himalayas. On the Tibetan side, on the north face, it is known as Chomolungma, with the same meaning as in Nepalese.

Lucifer, the light bearer was cast from heaven, because he longed to sit on the Holy Mount of God. He understood that the spiritual governance over the universe is executed on a mountain, and after his fall, he chose the summit of the Earth to establish his government on the planet. If God is the Father of all creation, seated on Mount Zion, then the devil would have to create for himself the title of mother or goddess of the universe, likening himself to the almighty and sitting on the roof of the world.

From this location, Lucifer could establish a worldwide Babylonian system of government. After the flood, he set his eyes on Nimrod, one of Noah's descendants, who became the first powerful man on Earth and the architect of the city of Babel.

Nimrod was influenced to establish an idolatrous system of worship to the sun, moon and stars in this city. This spiritual structure was designed to rule the kingdoms of the Earth and would employ governments, secret societies, and religions that would arise from it. He then set up the goddess Ishtar as the queen of the universe to accomplish this goal.

However, when the languages were confused, its inhabitants scattered, founding the nations of the Earth. They took the Babylonian system of idolatry and witchcraft with them to establish it in all the cultures that would evolve throughout history. And although the mother goddess would change her name with each civilization, her essence and origin would continue to be the same.

Every great religion that emerged out of Babylon utilized a system of idolatry and superstition, whose objective was to enslave its members through ignorance and fear. Even Israel, the people of God chosen to bring forth the Messiah, ended up corrupted by this system time and time again. In the Book of Revelation, Jesus calls this system, "Babylon the Great, the mother of the abominations of the Earth," from whom the kings of the Earth have all drunk her cup.[8]

Somehow, the Nepalese natives saw Everest, as the mountain where God could establish himself. As I researched its history, I realized that its first name was Deva-Dhunga, which means Throne of God. And even on the southern face, it is still known this way.

8) Revelation 14:8
9) The crowning of Queen Isabel II as monarch of the United Kingdom, Canada, Australia, New Zealand, South Africa, Pakistan and Ceylon took place on June 2, 1953.

Ishtar, the Babylonian goddess under the name of Sagarmatha, her Buddhist/Hinduist form, crowned herself to take the place of God.

It is also interesting to note that Edmund Hillary conquered Everest on May 29, 1953. The British crown sponsored his climb, and two days later, his prize was the great jewel presented to Queen Isabel II[9] during her coronation.

Edmund Hillary & Tenzing Norgay 1953

Somehow the crown of the mother goddess Sagarmatha strengthened the throne of the Queen of England. However, there was also a hidden curse, which sooner or later would require payment. Failing to understand the elements involved in the high mountains of the Earth can sometimes trigger fatal consequences.

Twenty-two years later in 1975, Sagarmatha demanded the life of Edmund Hillary's wife and daughter in a plane crash in Katmandu, the capital of Nepal.[10]

Twenty-two years after that, in 1977, as our expedition arrived into Everest, Sagarmatha demanded the life of Lady Diana,[11]the most popular woman of English Royalty and political daughter of the queen mother.

Later in this story, we will see how the number twenty-two plays an important role concerning what God would have us do in our confrontation with Sagarmatha. In fact, it was on a May 22nd when God spoke to us on the Popocatepetl volcano that we were to climb Everest.

Some may deem these mere coincidences, but there are hidden truths in a world foreign to most of the globe's population. An invisible, supernatural world that rules the natural one, together with its own rules and demands as well.

One year after receiving the call to climb the summit of the world, one of the greatest tragedies ever to take place on Everest occurred. A group of the most famous climbers in the world perished there. This disaster, recorded in books and which also made it to the big screen, was the stage that our feet would soon be stepping on. The pain, despair, terror, anguish and agony experienced by these able mountaineers would continue to pulsate in the deadly and stormy walls erected at base camp on the roof of the world.

It was clear that Everest was a mountain surrounded by curses, making it both grueling and deadly.

10) March 31, 1975 (44 years old) Nepal (Plane crash)
11) August 31, 1997

I believe that better understanding why I would embark on such a task as this is also important. What exactly was burning inside of me, driving me to face such a monster to the point of laying down my life for a people I didn't even know, in a region so foreign to my customs and me?

My Motivation

The call to deliver cities and combat the forces of the devil is the very essence of the gospel. This is what began to form in my heart beginning in the psychiatric ward, when I saw how the devil used pain to oppress and destroy mankind. This is the deep love of God for which He gave His most precious gift possible, His son, to redeem mankind from the destructive claws of the enemy.

Satan doesn't just engage witches and warlocks, but he fills the entire Earth with violence, aggression, murder, women beaten to death by drunken husbands, children killed in schools, young women raped by their own fathers, young people perishing from overdoses, hordes of individuals dragged by idolatry, living in sub-human levels of poverty, or victims of deadly diseases waiting on a wooden idol to deliver them.

Millions of children must run away from their homes because they can no longer stand the abusive beatings at the hands of a parent or their abandonment. Some leave their homes as young as two and three years old, perhaps rescued by a six-year-old sibling. Some dwell in sewers until they one day disappear, kidnapped by satanists and later sacrificed. Sometimes they remain silent, freezing to death on the street, clutching on to a younger sister just killed by a speeding car that fled away, No, it is not an exaggeration. There are countries that even slay children like rats because they no longer know what to do with them.

In the heart of every man, woman and child, there is an internal cry, silent to our ears, but exceedingly loud in the heart of God. It is a deafening cry, which once heard in moments of intense intercession, one cannot help but weep uncontrollably. This is what God hears every day, every hour. He listens to the cries of millions and millions of embryos that long to live but are hopelessly slain in abortions, in most cases because of their parents' desire to continue living in fornication and avoid responsibility. They are also killed by their government, as in China where women are forced to abort after their first child.

Beloved reader, do you know how great is the cry and pain of mothers who are forced to carry unbearable burdens, alone and deserted in life, or with spouses drowning in alcohol, vomiting on them, only to later want to satisfy their carnal desires with them.

Yes, God has allowed me to experience human pain first-hand in countless ways, by helping others. I have pastored in areas of darkness, with unimaginable levels of oppression and wickedness. A person would have to be made of stone, not to feel their heart shrivel, as they walk through the Brazilian fabelas or the poorest streets of India or Africa.

You can literally see the dead bodies of those who have starved to death lying on the streets. There are children gnawed by rats, in such unsanitary conditions that the stench makes it impossible to breath. When you walk through the atriums of the Hindu temples, the blood of animals flows like streams through the patios, as they offer up their babies to the powers of hell.

God hears the cry of this tormented world and every fiber of His being is moved by it. Can we really ignore how deeply God loves the world? Perhaps for some people, millions of individual perishing in hell is not that big a deal, but that is not the case of God's heart.

The heart of the Father feels the pain of every human being on the Earth because we are His children. Mankind is the affection of God's love. He loved humanity to the point of giving His Son to endure the worst suffering unto death, just to save us.

Every day, the Father sees His most treasured beloved ones raped, assaulted, murdered and tormented by the wicked atrocities evil can conjure. This takes place before Him day and night. Imagine just for a moment, what it would be like to see your loved one violated and butchered before your very eyes. This is what the heart of God feels when He sees the pain of the lost, all daylong.

Don't you think that Jesus is longing to see His army rise up clothed in His authority and motivated by His deep love and compassion?

Only those who truly understand the pain of God, and feel the affliction of those oppressed by the devil, down to their bones, will ever rise up and wage war against satan and his hosts, no matter the cost.

Spiritual warfare is risky, especially when it is done out of order, but God always keeps those who lay down their life for others.

The true love of Christ for every lost soul has been at the expense of the lives of many missionaries and their families. Yet that never kept them from journeying to the most perilous places to preach the truth.

The history of the true gospel is full of martyrs, men and women who gave up their own lives, even unto death, to establish the Kingdom of God.

Taking a stand against the darkness of their time cost Steven, Peter, James, and almost all of the apostles their lives, as well as the lives of thousands of other martyrs. I could fill entire books with the names of sons and daughters of God who loved a lost world more than their lives .

Spiritual warfare is the expression of God's compassionate heart , which will not rest as long as there is pain and wickedness on the Earth. This is what drives us to engage in the fiercest of battles, to bind and cast out any type of foe or power.

I made up my mind that there would be no room for the devil in my land nor in the nations God allowed me to wage battle. When God assigns me a nation, I will use all the power He has given me to stop the demonic forces from settling in.

My heart is filled with too much compassion and love for those in pain, to keep from waging war and giving my all for them. I also know that there are many others who will not be moved by the devil's intimidation tactics, because they also form part of the true army of God.

There are things that God does in the light to be seen by all, but there are others , which God keeps hidden, and these are the ones that bring about major changes.

There is beauty and reward in understanding, "the work behind the work." Perhaps King Solomon's fame by building the historic Temple will be admired for generations to come, but the question still lies, "What will be more valuable in God's eyes?" The one who set each stone or the one who received the plans from the Almighty One's hand, who in this case was King David?

Men tend to admire the visible things seen by the human eye, which are perishable. But God crowns His humble and faithful remnant with a never-ending glory, which cannot be seen by the natural eye.

The destiny of nations has not been entrusted into the hands of the rulers of the Earth, but they are in the hands of those who know God and whose intercession moves His hand to usher in His justice and light into the Earth.

First Expedition to Nepal

What I am about to share is not the expedition of great climbers whose experience, skill and physical strength led them to reach the greatest summits of the world. Nor is it the history of champions who left their names in the books of great achievements of man.

But this is a story about a group of inexperienced people who dared to believe God, against all odds, to take on one of the most daring and dangerous challenges ever known to man. This is the story of the living God manifesting and guiding us through the most extraordinary pursuit of our faith.

How everything began

As I meditated on how to accomplish such a great feat, exploring different ideas in my mind, I came across an amazing opportunity to measure my faith. One of our intercessors, which worked for Mexicana de Aviacion Airlines, 12 got two free tickets to India and then to Nepal, which is home to the world's greatest summit.

We hired a travel agency in India to help us secure a contact in Nepal, since no one in Mexico had the information we needed.

The story of the twelve spies who were sent by Moses to measure the possibility of accessing the Promise Land and identify every hurdle, came to my mind.

Of the twelve spies, only two, Joshua and Caleb, believed that God was greater than Jericho's towering walls and their dreadful army of giants. The rest only saw themselves as insignificant grasshoppers, incapable of winning.

Many of us may claim to have great faith, but it is only when we come against walls and giants in our life that we are truly able to discover if we are like Joshua and Caleb, or like the other ten spies.

Mt. Everest is a killer mountain that kills about thirty percent of its climbers. As far as the level of difficulty goes, it is an extremely technical mountain to climb, requiring great experience and expert high mountaineering skills.

12) Old airline who operated from Mexico at the time.

I had to be absolutely sure, not just of God's calling to carry out this mission, but also of the condition of my heart, my faith level and resolve to accomplish it. It was a daunting challenge, and simply assuming anything could easily turn into a death trap.

To start our journey, my friend and I went to Nepal's Embassy in Mexico City to process our visas. We immediately found favor with their personnel when we mentioned that we were organizing an expedition to Mt. Everest. The consul gave me an old book, written about the first expeditions to Everest prior to Edmund Hillary and Tenzing Norgay's conquering it in 1953.

The book contained pictures from that time period and described in detail the perils and challenges those first climbers had to face.

Just looking at those photographs made my heart stop. But no matter how ominous those images were, they would not deter me from traveling and experiencing it face to face.

My friend Silvia and I boarded the flight to New Delhi in December 1996. The travel agency picked us up and coordinated our arrival in Nepal.

They put us in touch with a Nepal Company called Kailash Himalaya Trek that specializes in these types of expeditions. They would take us to a hotel located in the Himalayas on this preliminary trip, where the Everest Summit could be seen from a distance.

After arriving in Katmandu and clearing customs, a charming Nepalese man, with slanted eyes and a full mustache, smiled at us while holding a sign with my name on it.

He was dressed in a simple dark outfit and sweater, giving him the appearance of a professional. His name was Santa

Subba, and He was the director of the company that was awaiting our arrival.

He had two colorful orange necklaces on his arm and quickly placed them around our necks to welcome us with great honor, as was the Nepalese custom. He bowed, placing his hands together, and greeted us with a traditional "Namaste."

After this wonderful welcome, he took us to an elegant hotel, which his company paid for as a courtesy. The following day, a helicopter took us to the small village of Namche Bazar, almost thirteen thousand feet above sea level. This is the most important commerce center in the mountain range, as well as the main village of the Himalayan inhabitants.

That evening we stayed at a mountain lodge, since the Everest View Hotel, from where the summit is visible, was not available during the Winter season. Mr. Subba also provided us with snow jackets and sleeping bags to spend the night.

It was quite an experience. We had never slept that way before, especially in the low December temperatures, which ended up freezing the crude beds made out of wooden boards.

The following morning, we met him for a delicious breakfast of eggs and curry with coffee, followed by a walk through the small Sherpa community. This is the name the inhabitants of the region go by, and it is a title they embrace with great esteem. Most men are carriers or expedition guides, while the women cook and tend to the small mountain shops. Their physical traits are like the Chinese, and their diet is greatly influenced by both Chinese and Indian cuisines. They are a very poor people, having to carry loads greater than their own body weight, just to make a few dollars. However, their kindness deeply moved us, despite the terrible conditions in which they lived.

In the afternoon, we went to the Everest View Hotel where they showed us the rooms and a large terrace where we could see Mt. Everest at a distance.

The site was indescribable. The peaks had a rosy, orange glow like a flaming fire or shining gold. I left Silvia at the hotel and looked for a solitary place to pray and gaze at the mountain we were assigned to.

I felt a great responsibility for the group, since we were all unskilled climbers and I didn't want to put their lives at risk over an impossible task.

I sat on a few rocks to the side and peered at Everest for over an hour. In the backdrop, one could see Everest's partly snow-covered mountainous made from smooth rock. In the natural, I felt like a gnat. Its rocky, pyramid-like form, both imposing and inaccessible, seemed to be glaring back at me as well. It was as if we were surveying each other, examining one another, like two rivals seeking to browbeat each other with a stare down. Who was stronger? Who would submit?

The more I stared at it, the greater my spirit grew. I knew well inside of me that to conquer any territory from a small venue to a large stadium, or even an entire city, I first needed to stretch out my spirit and join it to God's.

The presence of God started to grow stronger and stronger within me. Both my heart and spirit continued to grow as they were filled with His strength, and I felt an unbelievable amount of faith being imparted into me. God was infusing me with His greatness to the point of viewing Mt. Everest as something small and attainable. It was then that I knew it beyond a shadow of a doubt and stood up and yelled,
     -"You are conquerable! And I am coming for you!"

Filled with this conviction, I met up with my friend and host and asked him,

> -"What do we need to do to organize an expedition to Everest? I need a quote and a list of everything that we will need."

He just smiled and answered,
-"Well, first of all, this isn't a common expedition. The first thing you need is for the government of Nepal to grant you access. They only allow one expedition per route twice a year. I assume you are going to want to climb the South- East ridge, which is less difficult, and it's also the one that is most in demand. As far as I know, the next available opportunity is in 2010."

-"What? 2010?" I repeated in dismay. That was still fourteen years away.

-"It can't be," I thought. "That's impossible."
God would never be speaking to me about climbing a mountain that I would have to wait so many years for. After all, I was already forty-one years old and deemed it a great challenge at my current age. The news was beyond disheartening.

-"I'm sorry," he added. "It's not up to me, but, if you'd like, you may climb Anapurna or any other. They are also beautiful peaks."

-"No, Mr. Subba, it must be Everest," I quipped, completely frustrated.

That night I almost cried myself to sleep from the confusion. I was'nt understanding anything. Why had I traveled all the way to Nepal to return with nothing? Why had His voice been so strong and insistent, if the door was going to be shut anyway?

The trip back to Katmandu was a silent one. We were both very sad, including Santa Subba. In his mind, he thought he could sell us a climb to another mountain, but he soon found out that we only had one goal in mind. He left us at the hotel confirming that he would swing by later to take us to dinner.

In the midst of our heartbreak, we began to pray and seek clarity from heaven, but all we got was silence. We were perplexed, yet at the same time, there was something in us that refused to believe that God would have brought us so far just to tell us that the ascent was impossible.

That afternoon we stepped out and took a walk to get to know the spiritual atmosphere in Katmandu. The people were literally walking around like zombies with faces completely void of expression, reflecting the emptiness that resided in their spirit. Upon visiting the temples, we were horrified to discover people eating and communing with rats. They believed the rats were their gods. The temple of the goddess Kali, was the worst one of all. There were so many blood sacrifices offered to her that you could literally see a stream of blood flowing out of the sanctuary.

On the other hand, those whom they referred to as "holy men" were some scrawny looking, half-naked men who spent their days and nights smoking pot and watching over the holy sites.

We continued our walk arriving at the Baghmati River, that flowed at one end of the city. This was the site where people burned their dead and threw their ashes into the water. Those less fortunate, who could not afford to completely cremate their loved ones, would throw their half-burned bodies into the current. We constantly saw burnt or half-burnt corpses floating around in the river. The smell of burnt flesh made us shudder.

Observing these things broke us deeply, filling us with such compassion, and further fueling our resolve. We felt compelled to do something for them.

We were basically witnessing with our very eyes, all the horrors and suffering we had already surmised that these people experienced. Darkness controlled everything around them.

Sacred rats in the temples

We contacted one of the small Christian churches there. Every one of them was terribly persecuted and oppressed. There were no more than fifteen churches in the region and every last one of them were in deplorable conditions.

The suffering could be felt everywhere. Moreover, the despair over our powerlessness to see our mission come to fruition took a toll on us, filling us with even greater sorrow.

We returned to the hotel downhearted, meditating on everything that we had seen. Then around 5pm the phone rang.

> I answered. It was Santa Subba, and he sounded elated. -"Something has happened. I am heading to the hotel right now."
>
> -"Ok, great, what happened?"
>
> -"I must tell you in person. I'm on my way, wait for me!"
>
> -"What could have happened?" we asked ourselves, looking at each other perplexed. About fifteen minutes later, Santa Subba arrived, and we met him in the lobby.
>
> -"It's incredible. I could not believe it, when the fax arrived in my office." "What is it? Tell us!"
>
> -"We have just been notified of a cancellation of an expedition that was scheduled for next Fall, and they've given me the opportunity to offer it to someone else. I'm not sure if it is too short of a notice for you? You would only have eight months to prepare. What do you say?"
>
> -"We'll take it!" I exclaimed without hesitation. "What do we need to do to secure it?"

My heart beat with excitement and fear at the same time. After all, eight months was not that much time to get prepared and organize an expedition of this magnitude. It usually takes experts at least two years to properly train and plan for something like this.

-"Well, the first thing you need to do when you return to Mexico is to send me the mountaineering resumes of each of the climbers and a letter from the Climbing Federation from each climber's respective country, acknowledging each of you as a high mountain climber with all the necessary qualifications to climb Mt. Everest."

"Climbing Everest is like going to the Olympics. The government does not want neophytes going up there to die, they must make sure they are skillful and able climbers. Do you understand?"

"Furthermore, you are also going to need a letter requesting permission from the Nepalese government to move forward with the expedition, via the Khumbu Glacier route."

"I'll prepare a budget for you. Take into account that the government fee to accept the expedition is seventy thousand dollars."

-What does it cover?" I asked.

-"Nothing. It's just for the government permit to grant access to seven climbers. And it's another

ten-thousand dollars for every additional climber."
-"You must also calculate a budget of about four-hundred to five-hundred thousand dollars, which includes your team gear and all the expedition expenses, sherpas , guides and of course the government fee I just mentioned."

An internal battle began to wage within me nagging at my faith as these mountains of impossibilities rose like giants posing more of a challenge than the climb itself.

I took a deep breath and smiled with a sense of absolute confidence that everything would be taken care of, although on the inside, I had not the faintest idea of how to proceed.

-"Done deal!, Mr. Subba, as soon as I get to Mexico, I will get all those documents together and send them right to you."

Our vast climbing experience simply consisted of trekking the Popocatepetl Volcano, barely five thousand meters high, where crampons were not even needed. Where in the world were we going to get all those pre-requisites covered? And where were we going to get half a million dollars?

Conquering Mount Everest was more than a physical feat, but each challenge was more daunting than the previous one. Not only the expedition was almost impossible to achieve but also the spiritual battle we would have to undertake.

The endeavor was indeed enormous in every sense for people so void of experience and financial resources. Not to mention the time limitations we had to accomplish it all. But, there was one thing I was sure of; I wanted to know the God of the impossible opening the way and destroying any thought of limitation that might cross my mind. And this was that great opportunity.

During the flight back, I meditated deeply. The images of the immense, pyramidal black mountain tucked away in that inhospitable Himalayan range came to my mind over and over. The frightening photographs of the icefall became vivid in my rampant imagination. I felt transferred to the glacier, feeling the vertigo of standing close the abrupt icy cliffs. I felt so puny surrounded by those enormous and fragile ice pinnacles, called Seracs, threatening to crumble over me at any time. Hundreds had perished there, and their voices continued to howl, warning about the danger, making one feel their despair as they agonized.

One third of those who attempt to climb the mountain do not return.

-"What about us, Lord? Will we make it back alive?" I would ask within me, but all I heard was silence.

After reading this scripture several times I began to understand, "He who loses their life unto death, will find it, and he who wants to save their life, will lose it." Thus, fear of death had no part in this mission. Either we lay down our lives out of love, even unto death, or it was better to not even bother going.

The next question that came to mind was, "Who would dare to take this herculean step with me?"

Back to Mexico

Upon arriving back in Mexico, I began to seek God for a strategy to put together the documents required by the Nepalese government. I would think, pray, and go over and around every possible solution, but I did not even know where to start.

One night, I heard the voice of His Spirit speak to me crystal clear,

> -"Call the Mexican Climbing Club and speak with the director, and tell him the truth about this mission."

His instruction was just so strange for my rational mind. How was I going to tell someone who had no idea or notion about the invisible realm, that God was sending me to climb Mount Everest to topple the devil's throne that ruled from there? Not only that, but I didn't even have a clue about how to put on crampons. Surely he would laugh his head off at me.

-"Just do what I said!"
the voice within my spirit insisted.

I made an appointment and went to see him. We had rented some ice axes from him in the past when we climbed the volcano, and he had provided some great tips seeing that we were completely new to climbing.

-"How are you, Ms. Mendez?
How can I help you today?"

-"Well, ummm...I'm not sure if you'll understand, and perhaps what I'm about to say might sound strange. It turns out that there is a demonic force on Mount Everest and it has all the surrounding nations under its yoke. All those countries are suffering terribly. They are hungry and oppressed... and I...have a team that can deal with that. We have felt from God that we need to go up there and tear it down...and I need your help, not just to train us, but also with the Nepalese government that requires our mountaineering resumes and a letter from the Mexican Climbing Federation certifying that we qualify to climb up there...and I have no idea how to do it."

He grinned ear to ear and then laughed shaking his head from side to side.

I froze before the obvious sneer from someone who had no idea of what I was saying.

-"Please, don't take me wrong. I am not laughing at you. It's just that you caught me off guard and left me stumped. What you are talking about is one of the most serious issues with climbing Everest. There are even books that have been written with testimonies of climbers who have encountered dark spirits up there, and pressing on just filled them with more fear."

-"Listen..." he stressed, as he stood up and picked a book from his bookcase. He flipped through the pages for a moment and read a paragraph.

-"The British climber, Frank Smythe, who attempted to climb Everest several times in the 1930's, has the most colorful story. He describes an encounter with two presences, the first a benign one, which seemed so real, that it even offered him some of its mint cake. Later, he found strange objects floating in the air, one of which seemed to be squatting had what "appeared to be underdeveloped wings," while the other had a bump, like a beak or the spout of a kettle. They both pulsated interchangeably... emanating a type of horrendous semblance."[13]

"There are many stories like this, and as trainers, we don't know how to prepare climbers for them. And if you know what to do, you're really going to help us all." He then added, "If you had told me this ten years ago, I would have said it's impossible, but with teams nowadays, plus good guides and good high-mountain training, I believe it's possible."

13) Frank Smythe: The Six Alpine/Himalayan Climbing Books. Published by Baton Wicks. Pg. 634

-"So, you'll help us?" I interrupted, excitedly.

-"Well, slow down. I will help you, if you commit to an intensive six-month training and submit to everything I tell you to do. I certainly don't want to have your blood on my hands. If you agree, I will send in the application to Nepal along with the your resumes, and we must find a way to get the letter from the Climbing Federation. That won't be an easy task, but we surely can contact someone that can help".

-"Yes, absolutely!" We will commit to the training. When do we start? "How many would it be?"

-"Mmm...I'm not sure right now, but there's at least three of us to start."

-"Well then, get ready. I will meet you here on Friday of next week to pick up the equipment you will need, and we'll get started on your training a week from Saturday. I will get a quote ready, and I will speak to a couple of mountain guides to train you. You don't have much time, so you will have to work very hard."

I left with great joy and thankfulness to God for this initial victory. Although, I still didn't have a clue the people God would bring to form the team or how they would survive the training I knew He was putting the pieces together. Nevertheless, the financial mountain had grown a little higher. But there was one thing I knew for sure God had to do the work because in my own strength it was impossible.

The Challenge

Another thing to understand, is an expedition of this nature takes between five to six weeks. We had to transport everything we could need. Just to get to base camp, located at almost eighteen thousand feet high, one must walk around eleven days, going up and down mountains and valleys.

We needed a team of thirty Sherpa, between carriers, guides, cooks, and those building a fixed route at the Icefall. Furthermore, we would need tents at each one of the camps making a total of twenty high altitude tents. We would also needed sleeping and cooking tents for the Sherpas at base camp.

The kitchen would have to be large enough to feed over forty people three times a day, which also meant carrying a large amount of food, butane gas, and every type of utensils. On top of all of that, we had to get seventy oxygen cylinders for climbing the high-altitude camps and the summit and, they were only made in Russia.

All of this required a vast amount of organization, including arranging for sixty Yaks (pack animals) to transport everything to base camp.

Organizing all of this was Santa Subba's job. However, for us, the most important thing was that we needed climbers, men, or women of faith willing to lay down their lives for such an exploit. In addition, they must have the faith to withstand the onslaught this endeavor would entail.

Meditating on all this stretched my mind to its limits.

Added to all this was the financial challenge. We were just a small intercessory ministry in Mexico. How on earth were we going to get these funds? This was indeed one of our greatest faith defies.y para nosotros lo más importante, era que requeríamos de escaladores, hombres o mujeres de fe que quisieran poner sus vidas en semejante hazaña y que tuvieran la fe para resistir todos los embates que esto representaba.

Raising funds for evangelistic events or victims of disaster and orphans is not that difficult. You always find generous people willing to give to these causes. The challenge for us was to convince people to give and support a spiritual warfare mission on the summit of the world, made from a team in which none of the participants were experienced climbers.

First of all, we had to convince them that there actually was such a thing as spiritual warfare. Then we had to persuade them that we weren't going to die, but that we would achieve our objective of dethroning the devil from his general headquarters on the Earth.[14] All of this, after the great tragedy on Everest, that took the lives of several of the greatest, well-known mountaineers in the world.

---

14) Ephesians 3:10 His intent was that now, through the church, the manifold wisdom of God should be made known to the rulers and authorities in the heavenly realms. We have understood that it is the job of the sons of God to manifest the victory of Christ, dethroning the principalities and powers of darkness.

Moreover, in just eight months during intense training I had to believe for the impossible. We had to scale thirteen peaks, sixteen thousand feet high, as well as practice rock and rappel climbing. We also had to run ten kilometers a day, and in-between our summit climbing, we had to scale every fifteen days a thirteen thousand foot peak overlooking Mexico City.

Furthermore, I also had to pastor the congregation God had entrusted me with and cover my international preaching engagements as well.

The grace and favor of God were upon me, and little by little our team started to come together my disciples were the first. Veronica and Lencho, decided to take on the challenge and train with me. Veronica was like a daughter to me. She was working as my secretary, and I continually encouraged her to study and press for a life of excellence. Her brother, Lencho, was also a young man who loved God and helped out in the congregation.

My spiritual authority and friend Rony, with whom I had climbed the volcano, started to help me collect the funds. Each one of us began to hold meetings with business people from various places to share the vision with them. The money started to come in, though not at the rate we would have expected; nonetheless, we always ran into generous people.

very well known American prophetess decided to send letters to all the important ministries throughout the US and Latin America, decrying our initiative as something that was not come from God and must be stopped.

She was well known, and I was not, which instantly curbed all our support.

Even Rony hesitated and wondered, "Don't you think that perhaps she is someone sent by God to spare our lives, and that deep inside this is all just madness?"

Utterly convinced, I turned to him and countered,

> -"Rony, I am going to quote you to you. You are a genuine prophet of God, and you have always stressed that when God speaks to a prophet, they need not consult with human council. God spoke to you and He spoke to me, and we have also received a number of confirmations in the process. Had this negativism come from you, I would give it some thought, but God is not going to speak to someone who has nothing to do with us, nor that doesn't understand the first thing about the role that mountains play in the destiny of nations. We must remain steadfast. We knew that the enemy was going to attack us. This is too big and there are millions of souls on the line.

I'm going to present my case to Dr. Peter Wagner, who is the worldwide leader of the intercessory network. He's will be in Guatemala with Dr. Harold Caballeros, who leads the Latin American branch, and it so happens I have been invited to speak at that gathering."

-"You're totally right Ana, we must stay the course. I will be praying. Let me know how it goes," Rony answered, convinced that we must not hesitate.

God opened the door in Guatemala and I was able to meet with Dr. Wagner. I showed him powerful photographs of our high- mountain training and let him know that we were not taking things lightly.

He led the intercessory initiative for the 10/40 window and this subject was pivotal.

-"We will never succeed if we do not first take down the throne that is located on Mt. Everest," I told him deeply convinced. "You have over seventy million intercessors under you and this battle for that entire zone must be taken to a higher level in order to be victorious. I know that the prophetess that's opposing us is very dear to you, and that many honor her, but God did not call her to this mission, He called us. So, if God didn't call her why would He now be declaring the opposite about the matter?"

-"Her main concern is for your lives because if you were to die in the attempt, the Intercessory Network would be terribly marked, discouraging many others from pressing on," he replied, attempting to excuse her remarks.

I thought to myself, so her concern is with the network's well being but not our lives? But I stayed silent.

> -"Doctor, please, I urge you to take this project before the Lord. God isn't going to send us there to kill us, but even if that were the case, any victory for the least evangelized region of the Earth will bear much fruit and silence any opposing voice. And if God were to require our lives to win those souls for Christ, then wouldn't it be worth it, Dr. Wagner?"

> -"What the Lord revealed to Prophet Rony Chaves and myself is that the region would never be won, as long as the strong man is not removed. When God gives us a strategy to succeed, regardless of how difficult it might seem, should we turn it down just because our lives are at stake? How then can we go on doing the same thing and hope that He will back us up?"

> -"Alright, I will pray and let you know when I have a response," he kindly affirmed, and got up from his seat and said goodbye.

Everything now hung by a thread and could come tumbling down at any moment. However, that is the place where faith grows, where the road branches out from doubt or conviction, as we remained steadfast in what we believe. There is nothing more dreadful for a pioneer than the voices of fear from those who do not understand. There is always resistance from the status quo that rejects change and the possibilities of something new. However, if God is truly in this endeavor, then victory is assured.

Not even four days had gone by, when I received a phone call from Dr. Wagner.

> -"Can you come to Colorado Springs this weekend? We have decided to support you, and I have invited some of the most powerful intercessors in the world for the meeting." I almost fainted from the emotion.

> -"Yes, of course, I will be there. Thank you, thank you very much, Dr. Wagner" I jubilantly agreed.

An Unknown Enemy

I arrived at the Global Harvest Headquarters in Colorado Springs, where the building designed to house the "World Prayer Center" was almost completed.

Dr. Wagner and his wife, Doris, invited me into their meeting room greeting me warmly. There were major ministers from various parts of the world gathered there. Among them was George Otis Junior, the most important spiritual mapper at the time. A pastor named Lock Bahndari from Nepal was also there, as well as many others from Europe, Asia, and Latin America.

After hours of presenting the project and informing them on how they could help, we were able to secure worldwide intercessory support. Even Dr. Wagner's wife, at that time almost 70 years old, enthusiastically affirmed that she would also go all the way to the Everest View Hotel and coordinate a rearguard team of intercession.

She also added that two young people from their ministry would join our mountaineering team, and they would also be giving us five thousand dollars for the expedition.

As enthusiasm filled the room, George Otis Jr.'s face remained serious. There was something that worried him deeply. He finally stood up and approached Doris and me.

-"There is something extremely dangerous in that region besides the mountain!" he stated with a bit of irony. "That part of the world has some of the most dreadful warlocks on the planet, known as Chods. Very few people know about them. During one of my research studies, they allowed me to participate in one of their initiation ceremonies, and it truly was one of the strongest demonic possessions I have ever witnessed in life. The demons literally strip their victim entirely of their will and mental faculties, filling them with very high-level demons. Once possessed, they become the guardians of the glaciers and are seen walking around, half-naked on them. With a single word, they can rain fire from the sky or freeze a person to the point of killing them. You must be well prepared because the Chods are bound to find out about your venture, and then climbing Everest will be the least of your problems. How about coming over to my house in Washington State, and I'll show you some detailed studies that I have on them."

He then added, -"The other thing to bear in mind is that Sherpas are very superstitious just like the Lamas priests. If the Sherpas figure out your plan and realize that you don't submit to their gods and traditions, they will leave you stranded in the middle of the expedition. On the other hand, I did some additional research prior to this meeting... because I wanted to be prepared and be as useful as possible. You will inevitably have to make your way through the Tengboche Monastery by the Ama Dablam, Everest's great guardian mount. Every single expedition, without exception, must be consecrated to Buddha and remain under the Lamas' protection. I doubt that they will allow you to move forward without this vital requirement in their culture."

Doris and I looked at each other with great faith conviction, confident that God could help us bypass these dangerous foes, but the great question was how? Our steps had to be precise, without the slightest possibility for error.

-"Thank you, George," Doris added. "And thank you also for your invitation. We will go and visit you."

After the meeting, Doris gave me a book called "Into Thin Air" by Jon Krakauer. It was the story about the 1996 tragedy in Everest detailing all the necessary steps for an expedition. She suggested we all read it.

I returned to Mexico feeling very happy and shared the good news with everyone.

Countdown Begins

As the months went by, we grew in strength, knowledge, and faith to face this great challenge.

God had been training us to deal with major resistance, dangers, adverse situations, and fierce electrical and snowstorms, along with thirty-degrees below zero temperatures, mountain earthquakes and cliff rappelling.

In our last expedition to the Huascaran, atop the highest peak in Peru, we survived eleven avalanches that passed by on both sides of our tents, which were almost torn right out of the ground because of the strong winds. We could hear the avalanches rolling down the mountain all night. The hand of God was faithful to sustain us, as His angels fended off the giant bodies of snow that made their way towards our camp. God himself battled the blood-shedding powers that had scourged Peru throughout generations. From that moment on, the "Shining Path" guerrilla organization, which Peru had submitted to, began its downfall.

Weakened to the Extreme

When we climbed the Pisco Summit, to acclimatize ourselves for the Huascaran trek, we had to leave Lencho in a rural hospital after his lungs started to fill with fluid. We almost lost him.

Ana, Lencho & Veronica training on Mexicos' Iztaccihuatl's Volcano

We had to take him down the mountain in dense darkness amidst deep crevasses and tumbling rocks. We were completely exhausted after climbing for sixteen hours and pitching our tents to make summit by dawn. However, Lencho would not stop coughing. I asked a Swedish expedition pitched next to ours for help. And the leader quickly knew what it was.

-"Your friend has pulmonary edema and you must take him down off the mountain at once. If you don't, he will die. This is very serious."

Making our way back down was a challenge beyond human strength. Our legs had very little fortitude left and were shaking from weariness. We had to climb down the moraine, the zone where stones accumulated through years of landslides beneath high camp. The rocks were unstable and one wrong step could cause a mortal fall off the cliff. Both Eduardo, Rony's trainer and the guide who had helped us on the ascent, aided Lencho, while Veronica and I covered the back.

We arrived at the high vertical wall by the foot of the moraine. Most of the team barely made the climb pulling themselves up with a rope, but my strength had run out to even try it. I was left completely alone. I couldn't even hear their voices any more.

Fear grabbed a hold of me like a dark dreadful giant seeking to cripple me and leave me to die. Lencho's condition continued to get worse by the minute. They had to go on without me.

I didn't know what to do, no matter how hard I tried to pull myself up the rope, I simply could not do it. My arms had completely given out, and I slowly began to go numb from the cold. My heart, stricken, began to beat slowly.

Ana at Peru's Huascaran Mountain Peak

I encouraged myself over and over again,
-"His perfect love casts out all fear. His Perfect love casts out all fear."

And right when I was about to collapse, I heard Eduardo's voice,
-"Tie the rope around your waist! We are going to pull you up."

After much effort, they were able to hoist me up. The guide went ahead with Lencho, to get him off the mountain and to a hospital, as we remained behind trying to find the path down.

Upon returning to Mexico, the devil tried to stop me with every type of attack, weakening me to the max. Out of nowhere, I started to suffer fainting spells. The cardiologist stressed that it was due to a faulty heart. The "c" vessel reactor, which activates the adrenaline flow was impaired. Every time I exerted a great amount of effort, my heart would cut off the supply of this vital hormone, and I would collapse. After seeing this, the doctor strictly prohibited me from mountain climbing or participating in any type of strenuous exercise.

And that was not all, high-altitude training helps to acclimatize our bodies and it is vital for mountain climbing. Red blood cells store oxygen and multiply as we climb and descend at different altitudes. It's designed to provide a climber with the right amount of oxygen needed to survive in areas where the air is thin and devoid of this vital element.

My blood had gotten thicker with every climb, which was a good thing, since it would provide me with the necessary oxygen my body needed. But then three weeks before the trip to Nepal, out of nowhere, I ended up with anemia.[15] My oxygen levels significantly dropped, making it harder for me to breathe even in my own hometown of Mexico City.

---

15) Lack of red blood cells

In other words, all my preparation up until then had been for nothing. Out of the three of us, which had undergone the training, only Veronica was healthy but she was still a late teen.

The rest of the team was made up of seven servants of God, whom although they had the faith, still lacked the physical conditioning required. For example, Liliana, my best friend and an excellent intercessor, her daily exercise routine consisted of getting in and out of her car. Only Rony, and Eduardo his trainer, had developed a certain level of muscular and aerobic progress in the gym.

All this to say our team had been reduced to its greatest level of vulnerability.

I knew that satan would do the unthinkable to keep us from making it to Everest, but I was also aware that the idea of climbing the world's summit wasn't just mere enthusiasm or an Earthly glory trip. I had clearly heard the voice of God and determined that nothing or no one would stand in the way of this mission. And if my natural heart and blood gave out; I would climb it with God's heart. And His blood would be my oxygen.

In addition, despite a great number of intercessors and churches who had joined in this effort the financial support stopped. We had very little time left, and had run out of doors to knock for more funding. We still needed over half of the budget.

We already had all of our personal gear, tents, and plane tickets. Eleven of us would climb Everest and thirteen would remain at the Everest View Hotel praying for us.

I asked Santa Subba to reduce the budget as much as possible. We still needed the permit fee of seventy thousand dollars, and a big amount to cover hotels and some expedition expenses. We relinquished every type of comfort, to save money and were willing to carry our cross to the extreme for the sake of millions of souls. They were indeed worthy of any price we had to pay.

After studying the book Doris had given me, I learned there was a station named Gorak- Shep prior to arriving at base camp,. The government of Nepal hired Sherpas from this small mountain village to climb a fixed route on the Icefall for each season (twice a year). The book further mentioned that climbers were only charged a fee to use it.

As I read this, I was perplexed because our quote included a fifty-thousand-dollar charge to build a route out of ropes and ladders on that same Icefall.

I tried to contact our coordinator, Mr. Subba, to find out why he wanted to charge us that amount, if it wasn't needed. He started giving me the run around, looking for all kinds of excuses to justify the payment. That is when I knew something was awry, and that he was trying to cash in on our inexperience.

We were three weeks away from the trip, and we could not turn back now. We were also lacking the letter from the Climbing Federation. The oppression grew more intense, but so did the intercession. Sleepless nights seemed eternal, fighting against a demonic army that sought to intimidate us with fear and doubt.

The responsibility of leading a group of inexperienced climbers, who had never undergone high mountain climbing, weighed down on me like an enormous rock crushing me. Only God knew the terrifying scenarios I lived out in my dreams, imagining all kinds of horrifying circumstances that could befall us. The devil was using every weapon he could to dissuade me. Those terrible and fateful moments of the 1996 expedition seemed to scream out from Everest, causing me to feel what those great mountaineers must have experienced as they plummeted to their grave one after the other. Their lost bodies forever buried in the snow or laying on the gorge, awaited us to share their final moments, face to face.

Amid the struggle and desperation, I received an invitation to share about the project in Guadalajara, Mexico. It turned out that our hostess' son was a national rock climber champion and his best friend was one of the most well-known and highly regarded mountaineers in the nation.

They both called the Federation and convinced them to give us the letter, arguing that it would be the first time a Mexican woman would ever try to reach the world's summit.

Along with these internal and external battles came one of the most difficult moments I had every experienced. God had asked our lives even unto death with no guarantee of ever returning.

If there was anything more difficult than making this decision and laying our life down on the altar, it was having to say goodbye to our loved ones, not knowing if it was the last time we would ever see our children's loving faces. When they embrace you not wanting to let go, all the while imploring for your safe return. Or when they hand you pictures of them, with tears in their eyes and the words "Please come back. We love you, your children Ana and Pedro," penned on the back of them.

I also had to leave my twin sister who had suffered a broken hip in an accident. Sitting on her wheelchair, misty-eyed and lips quivering, she squeezed my hands bidding a farewell that at the same time wrestled with keeping me with her and instilling me with the strength to proceed. In those moments, I couldn't help but speak hope and encouragement that everything would be all right, and that they had nothing to fear, although deep inside, I really was not sure. My lips declared, "Of course I'll be back," but in my heart I knew it might very well be the last embrace and kiss I would ever give them.

The right answer to the most difficult requests God makes is what positions us in areas where the devil cannot reach us; because everyone who truly dies to everything in this world, will never be stopped nor overcome by anything.

The Moment of Truth

It was August 24th when we boarded the flight from San Francisco to Nepal. We left in faith, without any money, not knowing what awaited us, together with 26 pieces of luggage and equipment. Our sight was set on God, the general and chief strategist of this extraordinary mission.

The expedition felt shady, since I didn't trust Santa Subba's. I did not know where nor when his dagger of betrayal and abuse would reveal itself, but we would surely face it. Yet, I refused to believe that God would have done so much to make this happen for everything to dissipate like a mirage before our very eyes, because of a lack of money. We were placing our lives and everything we possessed on the line. Something had to happen, but we didn't know what or how.

My team and I had left one week prior to Rony Chaves and the rest of the group to make all the necessary arrangements for the expedition. The North American team, led by Doris Wagner, was scheduled to arrive two weeks later, once the climb to base camp had begun.

After thirty hours of traveling, we arrived in Nepal completely exhausted. Santa Subba greeted us with a grand smile, as if everything was perfect, and took us to the Everest Hotel in Katmandu. It was an old hotel, with an alleged five-star reputation, but was actually far from it. It was rather an icon, where most of the highly reputable expeditions stay in. It was also our last contact with a shower, restroom and electricity.

From the moment we arrived, we could feel the spiritual darkness that awaited us. We could perceive strong opposition in the air. There was an inner struggle waging in each one of us that is commonly felt before a great battle. Who would defeat whom? Where were the ambush sites and hidden traps located at that made the enemy strong? We had entered an inhospitable territory, foreign to everything we knew in the west. It was a country where speaking about Christ was prohibited and where countless thousands had never even heard of His existence.

That night, our room was filled with the glory of God and we saw angels descend with glorious armors covering our spirits. They were fashioned with the face of a Lion and an iron horn on its forehead, and were made of pure gold. The gloves had bronze nails. We had read all about these features in the Bible, but now, we were seeing them as a part of us.16 Divine peace flooded our souls, and we knew that we were on the brink of an experience the likes of which we had never imagined. It was the threshold of a great destiny unfolding before us.

The next day, following a well-deserved rest, we went out to pray in the city.

The pollution in the air, the noise of motorcycles and vehicles in complete chaos was a clear reflection of the darkness in the region. The city was full of temples and ancient palaces with sophisticated wood and stone embossments, which laid in stark contrast to the indescribable poverty of its inhabitants.

Hippies, hikers, backpackers and Buddhist monks could be seen everywhere as they blended in with beggars, carts pulled by bicycles, all kinds of vendors and the colorful tunics worn by Nepalese women. It was without a doubt, a picturesque scene to the eyes of any westerner. Over two thousand, seven hundred temples and other monuments could be found in the Katmandu Valley. Sculptured, polychrome wood, red bricks, and copper roofs are commonly grouped together into very small spaces.

The ancient city was remarkably oppressive. One could feel the demonic presence of its gods with infernal countenances.

---

16) Mic. 4:13 Arise and thresh, O daughter of Zion; for I will make your horn iron, and I will make your hooves bronze; You shall beat in pieces many peoples; I will consecrate their gain to the Lord, and their substance to the Lord of the whole Earth.
Rev. 5:5 But one of the elders said to me, "Do not weep. Behold, the Lion of the tribe of Judah, the Root of David, has prevailed to open the scroll and to loose[b] its seven seals.

On this occasion, we were unable to walk around undetected, because the powers of darkness knew perfectly well who we were, and could sense the eminent threat that was before them.

It was hard to breath. It felt like walking at night through a subway's lonely, dark tunnels in a full of filth and graffiti. The pagan temples served as a link between the Earth and satan's false heaven. You could feel the gaze of dark beings the likes of living gargoyles peering at us from the highest pagodas. The people in the streets, we came across seemed like they lacked a soul, walking about with a lost look in their eyes, and foreheads marked with a red powder symbolizing covenants they had made with their gods.

The pagan altars were littered with seed, flower and fruit offerings being eaten by rats and dogs, while women consecrated their children to false gods. The main plaza was a haven for hundreds of pigeons scavenging for food among trash and excrement left behind by their sacred cows. Together with the flapping of pigeons' wings, we could hear the wielding of daggers in the multiple arms of the goddess Kali, who was now aware of our arrival. Adorned with decapitated heads and thirsty for blood, she would make her unrest known from her dwelling place.

Without a doubt, there was a light that radiated from our invisible armor, since though we were dressed as common tourists we drew the attention of the Sadhus, the "holy men" of Hinduism. They were naked, covered from head to toe with a white powder that made them look like they had just come out of the afterlife. Their skin was stuck to their bones. The palms of their hands were blood red, and they wore colorful bead and flower necklaces. Their faces were marked with red and yellow insignias, reflecting the same dragon-like deformation of their gods. They seemed restless and agitated within their niches. People would come to seek after and worship them. They resembled more the walking dead, entrapped by hell itself. Some managed to leave their hideaways with much difficulty, staggering around like drunkards, leaning on their staffs. They looked at us, trying to focus their pot-laden gaze on us.

We felt the protection of angels with us. We cried for those lost souls and covered the area with the blood of Jesus Christ through our prayers. We could hear demons squirming as we walked by, like wild herds sensing an imminent earthquake quickly approaching. They squealed like scared rats.

We finally arrived at the stupa known as Swayambhunath. This ancient funeral monument stood upright as a giant guardian of the city on the highest hill. The huge dome jealously guarded the relics of Buddah. At the top of it was a tower with two enormous eyes in each side from which nothing could hide.

Swayambhunath Stupa

The Stupa's Eyes

It was already dusk when we started our climb up the steep and strenuous staircase lined with strings of prayer cloths, fluttering in the wind, that took their prayer requests to Buddha.

As we got to the top of the staircase, the two giant eyes in the golden tower, lit up by the setting sun, seemed to firmly stare back at us. There was hardly anyone there, except for a few monks dressed in their classic orange and maroon tunics, as well as a large number of monkeys and stray dogs. The only sound was the rotating cylinders surrounding the stupa, which the Lamas religiously rolled with their hands. It sounded like a harmonic sequence of bells and chimes that moved with the wind.

Below the giant eyes, the stupa's slope resembled a snow-covered mountain and the golden conifer tower on it was like an antenna connecting the entire region to the Himalayan skies.

When they saw us, the monkeys went into frenzy and jumped off the edges. The area was filled with altars and burning incense around the stupa. The monks were perplexed, pacing from one place to another, unaware of what to do to control the craze-filled monkeys.

It was very clear to us that the stupa served as a link between the swirling, holy mountains and the city.

Contrary to what the monks sought to achieve with their prayers, the smoke emanated from that location was like a fuming chimney from the underworld. The idolatrous rituals formed a dense web of darkness, inundating the city with filthy spirits and magic veils. The city was in bondage. The grime and filth the monkeys lived in was transmitted to the inhabitants of the Katmandu valley.

We prayed quietly and intensely, to change the spiritual atmosphere in the abominable temple that the people were unaware of until they were exposed to the true light.

As night fell, we returned to the hotel. We were hopeful to hear good news from those who were assigned the responsibility of raising more funds, in the United States and Latin America

The Expedition At The Break Of Checkmate

We ran into Santa Subba in the lobby, who informed us with a big smile, that the Nepalese Tourism Minister was expecting me the following day to welcome our expedition in the palace. Moreover, we also had to have the seventy thousand dollars for the permit.

My heart sank. Even if we could have raised the money, there was no way to have it the next 24 hours. I made several calls, but I always received the same response,

-"We have not been able to get anything, yet."

Discouragement plunged upon us like an avalanche wiping out everything in sight.

I told the team, "Let's pray, because God did not bring us

this far to turn back now." As a matter of fact, that phrase was part of a song we would sing at church. We started singing it to try and recover some of our faith that had been shredded to pieces.

As we sang those lines, we started to be filled with peace, and together with it the possibility of hearing God's voice above every other voice of despair that had bombarded us.

And right in that moment, I heard something on the inside that left me puzzled,

> -"Are you willing to go to jail out of love for the deliverance of the 10/40 window?"

> -"Jail in Katmandu?" That had to be the most horrible thing imaginable, I thought to myself, not even daring to bring it up with the team.

But that inner voice insisted, and I was sure that it wasn't a passing thought from my emotions.

So, I decided to go ahead and share it with the rest of the team. Everyone froze, but little by little we agreed that if it was the will of God, we would be willing to do it. Furthermore, we also decided that if it were to happen, we would leave Eduardo, Rony's trainer, out of it. That way, we would be able to communicate with the others since he spoke some English.

Once we laid our freedom down on the altar, we continued to pray, and then I heard,

> -"Write a check for seventy thousand dollars, even if it has no funds to back it and give it to the Minister tomorrow. Don't plan on what you are going to say because I will open your mouth and fill it."

> -"No, that cannot be from God! It's embezzlement! There's no way that God operates this way, " I screamed inside of me interrupting the voice in my conscience.

> -"It's me! Your Lord! He exclaimed almost audibly. "Just trust in what I am telling you."

I knew that I recognized His voice, and it was definitely Him. His illogical command was wrapped in an indescribable peace and faith that flooded my heart with fire and faith.

After sharing this utterly mad proposal -or at least crazy from my standpoint- the rest of the team seemed convinced that it was a great idea, and that if God was going to open my mouth, then there was nothing to fear. Although, I still was not clear on the question He had asked about going to jail.

The next morning around 11:00 AM, Santa Subba stopped by to pick me up.

We arrived at the palace, an old, unkempt building, as is the case of most third-world bureaucracies. The office of the Minister of Tourism was one of the main areas. An officer opened the giant door that led to the Minister's spacious office, where he stood at the far end behind his desk, elegantly dressed in a Hindu suit with a gray mandarin collar and a small oval-shaped, which was common Nepali apparel.

If we were to succeed with the expedition I told Mr. Subba needed to speak exactly what I spoke. I knew that God would speak through me, and Subba needed to be precise. As I stepped into the office, my mouth opened, and before I could come up with a single thought I blurted,

> -"As Lord of Hosts lives in whom presence I stand, I greet you"

Mr. Subba, my interpreter, was dumbfounded. He hesitated a bit, but interpreted the greeting exactly as I had instructed him to.

In that moment, the room was filled with the presence of God. I was the first to be taken aback by what I had been declared. These were the same words that the Prophet Elijah used to greet King Ahab in the Bible.

As I uttered them, I could feel that same power accompanying me and filling me with courage and confidence.

The Minister frowned for a moment, thinking, "What manner of salutation is this?" but something supernatural overtook him, as he sighed and welcomed me.

-"Welcome, Ms. Mendez. We are very happy to have a Latin American expedition....please have a seat," he said with great courtesy. "I assume you brought the money for the permit," he continued.

-"Yes, of course. Here it is, Mr. Minister," I replied as I handed him the check with insufficient funds, which he received with a great smile.

Once again, words escaped my lips that seemed shocking to everyone.

-"Don't be too happy yet, Mr. Minister. That check does not have any funds."

His face became enraged as he stared at me like someone who had just insulted him.

-"Allow me to explain," I told him interrupting his gesture.

-"I am a servant of the Most High God; the Creator of heaven and Earth who has sent my team and I to climb Mount Everest. The reason is to deliver your nation and the surrounding areas from the oppression, the poverty and the suffering they are experiencing."

-"There, atop the mountain, are the forces of darkness that are keeping your country from progressing. And I have the only team capable of facing a challenge as defying as this. I gave you this check to give you legal right to throw us in jail after climbing Mt. Everest. Climbing it is a divine command that we must obey. I say this, to let you know how much I believe God is sending us, and how much I want to help your nation. We are even willing to lay our lives and freedom to deliver your country from the oppression it is under."

I continued,
-"This is what my team is willing to do for Nepal, and displays the level of love we have for your people. But you Mr. Minister, what are you willing to sacrifice for your country?"

I paused and then added,
-"I came to ask you for permission to make the ascent without the cost of the permit because we have no money. We are here believing God and paying a high price for doing so. We are not seeking fame or human glory, but because of our love for you and your nation."

He fixed his eyes on me paying close attention. He was skeptical on the one hand, but also moved by my conviction on the other.

-"What I am about to say to you, is God speaking directly. If you grant us this permit, Nepal will enter into a commercial agreement with South Korea that will transform the financial future of this country. If you deny us the permit..., then the following will happen, which is not the will of God:

The Lord says that 'the fire is beneath the ice,' and you will see blood running through the streets of Katmandu. Bear in mind that this is not a threat, but simply the truth of what will happen."

There was silence in the room. The Minister sighed deeply and nodded his head as he handed the check back.

-"There's no way for you to know this. I just left a meeting with the Prime Minister and a revolution is forming against the kingdom. Their slogan is, "the fire is beneath the ice."

He then added,
-"I want to help you, but I cannot make this decision alone. Give me five days to speak with my counsel and I will let you know."

-"Mr. Minister, with all due respect, you know the first week of October is the window to make the climb. If we do not leave for Lukla tomorrow for base camp and acclimatize, we will lose that window. If you cannot grant us the permit, then at least don't hinder us. Mr. Minister, tomorrow we will leave so we appreciate that you will do what you can."

-"I will see what I can do, but I cannot guarantee anything." "Thank you, Mr. Minister."

As we left, I instructed Santa Subba to have everything ready for the following day. The expedition would begin, and God would be with us.

Troubled with everything he heard and unsure of how everything would turn out, Santa Subba simply shook his head from side to side and agreed to handle everything.

There were several government checkpoints on the access route that had to verify that all our documents were in order. There was also a mandatory four-thousand-dollar deposit that guaranteed climbers would bring back their trash. And of course, we didn't have that either.

We will never really know what happened with the minister and the checkpoints, but the truth is that we never really passed by any checkpoint, nor were we forced to leave the security deposit for the trash. Either God transported past the stops or we were invisible to the checkpoints. The truth is we are the only expedition to attempt a climb on Everest without making a single payment or showing a single document . We were later told it was impossible for the government to allow an expedition on base camp without a permit.

On the other hand, history tells us the Communist Revolution that secretly started in 1996 burst out right after our visit, obtaining the final victory in 2005. This is when the Nepalese kingdom was overthrown and it became a republic. The fire truly was beneath the ice!

Everest

Part 2

8

En Route

Early the following morning we headed towards the airport. An old freight helicopter awaited us filled to the brim with packages, supplies, duffel bags, and all types of high mountain equipment. There were no seats for passengers, so we had to sit wherever we could, amidst the expedition cargo.

Upon takeoff all manner of civilization and comfort was left behind. The amazing mountain range majestically unfolded as an elegantly intimidating picture that we had been sent to conquer. Its enormous peaks stood out amid the morning fog that began to dissipate as we made our way into the Gorka mountain region located in the Dudh-Khola valley.

The giant masses of rock and snow formed a narrow passage through which the pilot maneuvered . At a distance, we caught a glimpse of the runway at Lukla's rudimentary airport, which came to an end in front of an enormous stonewall.

This was the small town where most of the Sherpas lived and from where all expeditions departed. It is located 2800 meters above sea level. Basically, it was just an airstrip surrounded by houses, low-end restaurants, and basic hotels.

The trek towards base camp would take about eleven days. Since the beginning of commercial expeditions in 1998 many improvements have been done to the route. Mountain tourism has been growing and as a result, shelters and restaurants along the way have greatly developed. However, during our trip it was still very rustic.

After the beautiful walk by the river side, crossing hanging bridges and enjoying the ravine valley, was the climb to Namche Bazaar. We had descended three to four thousand feet to cross the river. Now we had to climb a slope about three plus thousand feet high among steep precipices.

One of the most difficult points was a hanging bridge about 300 feet high with some of its boards rotted.

One of many hanging bridges we crossed

There were two intercessors in our group that were going to stay in a shack across from the Everest View Hotel. One of them, Silvia, was almost sixty years old, and her sluggish pace slowed down the entire team. We only had one guide with us. He was a young, pleasant and helpful Sherpa whom we decided to call Jose, since his Nepalese name was hard to pronounce. He loved the Latin name we gave him.

To him, climbing up to this point was a quick hike he could easily achieve in less tan three hours. Unfortunately, the amount of stops, to allow the oldest members of our team to catch their breath, turned into a sixteen hours journey. Night fell, and with it the rain. None of us had flashlight since the guide never imagined it would take us so long. He decided to leave us along the path while he climbed aheadt to get some lamps. We were alone, in total darkness, knowing there were abrupt drops all along the way, we could not see in any way.

We began to sing to stop fear from ensnaring us when something amazing and supernatural occurred. A pail blue light began to glow from our bodies, lighting our way. It was something glorious we had never experienced.

That is how we managed to make it most of the way. As we drew close to the city, we saw Jose running towards us. He was surprised that we had come so far in the dark.

3380 meters above sea level was the town of Namche Bazaar described as the doorway to the High Himalayas. Every hiker in the Khumbu region must visit this site on their way to other ones, since it is the most important commerce area in the region.

Namche Bazaar

Tras una merecida cena continuamos el ascenso hacia Shyangboche que se encuentra a tres mil setecientos sesenta metros de altura. Era un punto clave para la aclimatación y donde pasaríamos algunas noches esperando al resto de los equipos.

After dinner, we continued our ascent toward Shyangboche, located approximately 3700 meters above sea level. It was a critical point for our acclimatization where we remained for several nights as we waited for the other teams.

We stayed in a small cabin , which lacked basics necessities such as water, electricity and restrooms. It consisted of an open area with two rooms and a few boards to place sleeping bags. There was a brass and iron chimney to warm ourselves using dried-manure yak as fuel, and a humble dining room in the center. How our tired and aching muscles longed for a hot bath, but after two days of walking we had to settle for a few hand wipes.

The following day we found a place that rented showers. It was a small room made of wooden boards, not more than a square meter, with a bucket of hot water on a shelf and a hose to shower. But it was a gift from heaven for us just to feel a tiny trickle of water on our body. Unfortunately, I didn't think about taking a towel on the expedition, mistakenly assuming that the hostels along the way would provide them for us. Grave mistake!

Jose, our beloved Sherpa, let me use his towel, which he hadn't washed in at least a month. But if that was my only option, then I thanked God for it.

Having pampered our bodies with the blessing of personal hygiene, we proceeded to organize some of our things. One problem was the prayer flags, Buddhist Sherpas placed for protection in areas where we slept for more than one night. They used these to consecrate the expeditions, ensuring the best of luck for everyone on it.

In the center of each prayer flag, you could find a "lung ta" (a strong horse) with three flaming jewels on its back. Ta is a symbol of speed and of transforming bad luck into good luck. The three flaming jewels symbolized Buddha. The square flags included different versions of over 400 written mantras, designed to be invocations that connect them to diverse deities.

There was no way we were going to allow a web of invocations around our camp. This was a pivotal factor, just as important as the mission itself. The pureness and precision of Christ would not be superseded with superstition and prayers to foreign gods. For some, this detail might seem irrelevant, but not to God since it was a mission aimed at taking down the devil's headquarters on Earth.

Many people today tend to gravitate towards oriental religions as if they were a source of light. And though it is true that some of their ethical principles are extraordinary, their fruit nonetheless is devastating. The tree of good and evil is full of good on the surface, but its end is full of death. This is exactly what is projected and produced by those individuals who devote themselves to these practices. If heaven was attained through meditation and ethics, Christ's death and resurrection among the dead would have been in vain.

Having anticipated this situation prior to the trip, we made our own flags just like the Buddhist ones, but with Biblical verses in Spanish. We brought an entire suitcase full of stringed flags that we presented to the Sherpas as a gift of love.

> -"We have made these flags with great love with our own hands and prayers, just like you do. It is a way of showing how much we love you and want to identify with your customs," I added as I handed the flags to Jose.

He was visibly moved as he accepted them with gratitude, placing them around the cabin as was the Sherpanese custom. To them, as is the case with many religious followers, rituals are no more than superstitious formalities which the majority do not identify with. All that mattered to them was for the expedition to be blessed by one god or another.

The Sherpas' respectful attitude towards our faith, allowed us to see into their dire need for a genuine encounter with their Creator. They were always amazed when God would do something for us.

We had to spend three nights in Namche Bazaar waiting for the rest of the mountaineering team. We used those days to acclimatize our bodies to the altitude, consecrate the territory for Christ and engage in strong moments of intercession.

First Great Battle

We were in a small meadow that stretched out in front of the lodge. It was a strategic location, set between great snowy peaks that faced directly towards Mt. Everest. We still had not been able to see it because it was always covered by clouds.

On the afternoon of the second day, while in prayer, an army of demonic beings came to oppose us. The spiritual realm opened up and we could see with our natural eyes. They were the guardians that protected the devil's great throne. The most intimidating figure of all was a winged creature, like a dragon with the face of a gorilla covered with exacerbated features.

The sky turned black, demons took the shape of dark clouds in the likeness of jackals and wild beasts standing on the summits of the mountain range.

The mountains, which are normally made up of rock masses in the natural, took on the form of the faces of the entities that possessed them. They were true giants rising up to assist the spiritual forces that sought to stand against us.

We remained calm and allowed our spirits to be permeated by the greatness of our omnipotent God. Even in our minuteness, we still knew that we were greater than they because God was with us.

We retaliated in intercession, worshipping and exalting the power of God to destroy our enemies. Droves of angels descended from Heaven to aid us. The battle could clearly be felt in the heavenly realms. Angels would battle the hoards of evil clothed by the grotesque cloud formations, while the sky lit up with intense lightings and thunders that shook the mountains. The thunders' echoes bounced off the gigantic rock formations making it a truly chilling encounter.

I literally felt like the Lord Jesus, in His manifestation as the Lion of the Tribe of Judah, took hold of me, His spirit and mine were clearly one. The winged, dragon-like demon came after me. I could feel how my spirit clashed against it, violently shaking my body. Not only had my spirit grown, but my golden armor as well. I felt as the bronze claws God had given us, dug into the body of that fierce beast. Its sharp nails sought to pierce through my armor but to no avail. For a moment he struck me to the ground with a blow, as I also fell physically. His hideous jaws opened up before my countenance, and it was then that I let out a powerful roar and managed to get up. The blood of Christ in me manifested emitting powerful rays of scourging light, tossing the creature far away from me.

I shouted the name of the Lord with all my strength and fire from the Almighty descended burning him up.

The demons that remained started falling by the dozens, as the sky opened up and a glorious beam of light shone upon us. The mounts once again took the form of mountains, but we now knew what they hid beneath. There was no doubt that they would regroup and renew their strength as our expedition advanced...but how and when will they attack? That was the great question.

We were exhausted but pleased with the unmistakable victory God had granted us. We fell on our faces, worshipping God and giving Him thanks. The true war had begun, and we had won our first battle.

Great Embarrassment

Two days later, after the rest of the team had joined us, we headed towards the monastery of Tengboche, leaving those who would make up our rear guard behind.

The trek was one of the most difficult ones, since we had to descend about fifteen hundred feet to climb a rugged two thousand feet slope at twelve thousand feet above sea level.

We stopped to eat lunch at a rustic café on the way, where members of a Spanish expedition came to greet us. They were also attempting to climb the summit of the world.

-"You must be the Latin expedition," one of them jeered in a Spanish accent. "Everyone at base camp is expecting you. There is great expectation about your arrival."

-"We had no idea they were waiting for us," replied one of our team members opening the conversation.

-"Oh yes, the Latin camp is the largest of them all, so they are very interested in meeting you."

After speaking for a while longer and rehydrating ourselves, something came to light in the conversation that stunned us.

To better understand what happened next, we must explain what had taken place weeks before our arrival. A group of Sherpas, sent by Santa Subba, had gone on ahead to set up the tents, dining rooms and kitchen at base camp, just like every other high-altitude camp. This is the norm in any expedition.

-"But what has everyone a little concerned," continued the leader of the Spanish expedition "are the path of fixed ropes that you had the sherpas build on the Icefall. It looks more like a roller coaster in the middle of a glacier," he added in a mocking tone.

-"The truth is that the route built by the government is exceptional this year and it's in a straight line."

My face went from rage to embarrassment. We were the laughing stock of all the other camps. Santa Subba had built something ridiculous just to charge us the fifty thousand dollars, and now it was obvious that we were totally inexperienced and had been taken advantage of by our organizer.

The Spaniards were sympathetic towards us and joined in our resolve to fight the injustice perpetrated against us. It was the beginning of a beautiful friendship that continued to develop throughout the expedition.

We resumed our climb up the slope, when a messenger arrived with a letter sent by Mr. Subba. The letter warned that if we didn't pay him the rest of the bill, he would kidnap Doris Wagner and the intercessors that were set to arrive by helicopter at the Everest View Hotel in Shiangbohe the following day.

I asked the messenger for the walkie-talkie and contacted the intercessory team we had left behind. I asked them to send Doris a message in Katmandu warning her of Santa Subba's upcoming attack. Then, I sent him a message that we weren't going to pay a dime for the ridiculous route he had built on the Icefall and to stop taking advantage of us and act like a professional.

The messenger left, but I stayed behind feeling disheartened. I didn't want to scare anyone with the threats in the letter. We continued climbing the steep slope, but the devil caused me to lose my focus completely. My mind kept on thinking on the kidnapping and on every kind of negative idea that Santa Subba could muster to foil the expedition.

And to make things worse, a wave of darkness quickly approaching from the monastery only worsened my fears and frustration. I could not concentrate. All of a sudden, my soul felt overwhelmed and distressed. I had been bearing too many things, including months of struggles to raise the funds and the intense dangers during training. I was further burdened by the responsibility of leading inexperienced people unfamiliar with everything having to do with mountaineering. I didn't even know if Lencho, who had nearly died at the Huascaran peak, would be able to handle the heights this expedition required. My heart started to beat slowly as I felt a lack of adrenaline in my body.

The opposition was fierce, and several team members had started to experience high altitude sickness, dizziness, and nausea. Some were talking about turning back, but it was too late to return. The best option was simply to press on towards Tengboche.

I had to pause, withdraw from the rest of the team and pour my heart out to God in tears. The load on my shoulders was just too big. I knew that my faith served to encourage the team and that they needed me, but I was falling apart. I could imagine feeling a little bit like Moses, the great hero of faith. Israel's deliverer was trapped between Pharaoh's army and the Red Sea, with hundreds of people yelling,

-"You brought us all the way here to die!"

After shedding some tears, I began to draw strength from within, for I knew that together with God's heart, we would have the strength to overcome every obstacle. I had to silence every lying word running through my mind until all that was left was the voice of God.

Right at that moment, a woman walked passed me with a load that was larger than her. Her eyes reflected the brokenness within her soul. She had no dreams, no hope for a better life, giving her all for a few measly dollars that were barely enough to survive. For a moment our eyes met, and I once again focused on our cause. Our climb was for our love for them. And her pain and her burden were visibly greater than mine.

God truly does speak in extraordinary ways!

After that encounter, God's peace and strength filled me once again. I decided to forget about Santa Subba, the money, and anything that wasn't a part of my main focus of delivering the 10/40 window. I shook off the enormous burden that oppressed me and reunited with the rest of the group.

-"Everything alright?" asked Rony.

-"Everything's fine. Let's keep on going."

Rony Chaves and José

The Thengboche Monastery

There were altars all along the way, as well as prayer flags consecrating every pinnacle on the mountain trail.

As we neared Tengboche, the darkness became more and more dense. One could hear in the distance the sound of ceremonial bells summoning the monks. This was the site where the Lamas jealously guarded the heights of the Earth. A great number of crows restlessly fluttering about came to witness our arrival.

Before us, the great Ama Dablam, Everest sentinel and sacred mount protector of the monastery, rose like a giant eye watching us. Its elongated and coniferous form seemed more like an enormous bird keeping close guard of everything.

It was about four in the afternoon when we arrived at the shack on the mountain facing the cloister.

The monastery served as an enormous speaker for the mantras and repetitive sounds of its bells of invocation, that weaved a giant shroud extending throughout the mountains. It was either going to be a spiritual door that would grant us access to continue, or a pit to the most dreadful of ambushes.

We prayed and worshipped intensely until we decided to enter the monastery, while others remained as the rear guard.

It was built as a small replica of the Lhasa monastery in Tibet. It had three main floors painted with lime, filled with some windows and wooden shutters that were shut, while others were in the shape of a pagoda. On the front portal, facing a great stone staircase that gave way to the enclosure, stood two roaring lions and dragons carved out of wood.

Thengboche Monastary

We quietly walked in as the crows croaked and flew from side to side, restless and scared.

The smell of burnt wax and incense permeated the hallways. It was bad enough to have to withstand the height at four thousand meters, but now we also had to endure the imbued smells on the old wood-covered walls.

We had to see beyond what was visible and human, beyond empty religions that trapped men in a cycle of death and superstition as they sought to reach for something they would never attain. This was written on one of the drawings in the inner murals depicting men continually struggling with a chastising God and a demon from the pit of hell which decided what cycle they would remain trapped in, lifetime after lifetime.

One of the Lamas followed our every step, as a keeper who wasn't about to allow anything to disrupt their sacred ceremony. Liliana smiled at him with her beautiful countenance, and in order to distract him, she asked him to lead her to a restroom so we could make our way in. She was skillful at drawing attention and was able to lure the guards far away from us.

We reached the main chamber where the monks practiced their meditations. They were lined up in rows, about twenty of them dressed in their traditional reddish, brown and orange tunics. Their silence was interrupted by a sudden ringing of bells, together with the singing of their mantras, which sounded like a noisy beehive.

They all bowed in one accord before a giant statue of Buddha surrounded by hundreds of lit candles. The entire hall was filled with colorful drawings and carvings made from varnished wood. There were dragons everywhere, as well as wide-eyed demons and lions with open jaws. A number of grotesque gods with knives and other diverse weapons could also be seen around the room.

Rick, one of our North American climbers and I, were able to infiltrate the ceremonial compound. They didn't seem to mind our presence making us even bolder.

Statue of Buddha Inside the Monastery

We knew that the sound they emitted was very important to preserve the cloak that safeguarded the mountains, and we needed to interrupt it somehow.

We waited for them to start their chanting anew, and at that point we released a very high- pitched note, like a sword of sound in the midst of darkness. It was the sound of the light of Christ coming out of us. Even though what we were doing was difficult to perceive in the natural realm, spiritually it caused great commotion. The monks broke their concentration and moved about confused.

In the end, it's not what we do, but whom we are that truly manifests in power. Things that might sound childish and incomprehensible to the natural mind, once saturated with faith, cause heaven to break open in the midst of any circumstance.

The rest of the team surrounded the sanctuary on the inside and outside, setting up angels to arrest the Lamas in time and space, so that our expedition could go through unnoticed by their natural senses.

When we left, the skies had closed up once again. God commanded us to leave that place, even if it meant at nightfall. We instructed Jose and the other guide that had joined us, to press on towards the next shelter, which was still three hours away.

Climbing that never-ending slope had taken us over eight hours, add to that the condition that most of the climbers were in was more than anyone could endure. However we all clearly understood that it was imperative to leave that area.

The spiritual atmosphere was disheveled, and the enemy continued to dangerously stalk us. The sky had been filled with black clouds and the Ama Dablan was covered with a thick fog, which fell along the way.

It's very likely that the Sherpas and carriers with us might have thought that by entering the monastery, we had received the Lamas' blessings for the expedition. But truth be told, the monks never forced anything on us to consecrate us, nor did the Sherpas ever ask anything about it.

This had been a great victory since it was a vital and determinant step so the Sherpas could move on.

By the time we arrived at the following shelter in Deboche, we were completely exhausted. The primitive lodge consisted of a hall with several rooms separated by wood sheets that reached halfway and 2 boards per room to place the sleeping bags on. None of the mountain shelters had toilets or showers. If one needed a bathroom at night, bowls or bottles were used and then dumped in the morning.

That night we fell asleep completely worn out. However, at about three o'clock in the morning, a noise and an oppressive presence suddenly awoke me. There were two semi- nude, cadaverous men inside my room. Their bodies were covered in white powder and their eyes out lined in red paint around, which made their eyes appear black. It was the Chods, George Otis Jr. had warned us about.

I will never forget the look of death and hatred in their eyes as they stared back at me. They mumbled strange words that could have been a spell. They had come to kill us.

> The Holy Spirit quickly instructed me.
> -"Manifest your armor!."

In an instant I saw myself with the face of a Lion, a horn of iron, arrayed in gold with bronze claws. I stood up in front of them, boldly raising the claws with authority, and then I roared like a lion. Upon seeing me in this form, they were filled with terror and disappeared into the night.

We realized that many of the temple guardians, both in Katmandu and Tengboche, had similar colors in their armor. They were golden lions, standing, with a Pegasus-like horn on their forehead, and claws extending towards the front.

In God's wisdom, He had clothed us with His own symbols similar to the Tibetan guardians, which ended up terrifying and confusing them.

The following morning, we were able to contact our rear-guard team in Shiangboche. Nowadays, it is easy to communicate from the shelters. There are cellular phone stations and WiFi, but back then radio was the only form to get in touch, and even then at certain times of the day and only from certain locations. Doris had sent word that neither her, nor her intercessors, some who were more advanced in age, would allow themselves to be menaced by Santa Subba, and would board the helicopter as scheduled. I felt at ease with the victorious attitude they had embraced.

The Sherpa Graveyard

The next few days consisted of intense treks, about ten to twelve hours per day, until we reached base camp. On the way, we had to pass through a gloomy graveyard, where the gravestones of all of those who have died on Everest lay, both climbers and Sherpas. Their bodies had either been covered by avalanches, landslides or had been shattered in the precipices. No one brings down the bodies from the mountain of those who perish, so this place serves more as a memorial.

In fact, this was part of the emotional training we had to work through, since we would have to walk by frozen corpses, or perhaps even over them, if they were located in a compromising position on the mountain.

The location of the monument to the dead was also quite striking. To think that one-day, these fearless climbers passed by this same place, but never came back, shook us to the core. Flowers, prayer flags and offerings decorated the memorials, in the form of piles of rocks. It was a clear reminder that beyond that threshold, the mountain would decide who lived, and who died.

When I think of the high summits of the earth, I see them like petrified pride draped in a grueling and dictatorial majesty that decides who is welcomed and who is not.

Arrogance, boastfulness and vainglory will get you to a certain point. But those that live are the ones who understand that one can only climb with the deepest humility, or by making voluntarily or involuntarily covenants with the darkness that inhabits them.

The Sherpas passed by there with great reverence to their dead. The summit, where the graveyard was located, also served as a place to rest and replenish one's strength.

We were at five-thousand meters above sea level and the height was starting to take it's toll on our bodies. We all took time to meditate and think about how we would enter, what is known as the zone of the shadow of death. From that point on, there was no vegetation or sign of life, just crows circling the mountains.

Predestination

The Periche valley, we had just passed below, had a very strong effect on me. It was as if I belonged to that place. It was in my bones and in my blood. Ever since I was a little girl, there was a painting in my house, which had always caught my attention, of a beautiful landscape painted in 1897. No one knew where that beautiful valley, which the painter had so preciously depicted in such detail, was located. It was a mountainous place with low clouds that covered its summits. There was a beautiful valley in the center showing a pond where a herd of small, longhaired cattle drank. They were yaks, surrounded by a grassy field strewn with small red and yellow flowers.

Exactly one hundred years after this painting was made, I was walking through it with my own two feet. It was a painting of the Periche Valley. It was as if something that had been lying in wait a whole century was connecting with me. Something was being given to me from eternity, and it had led me all the way over here, across the globe, to receive it. A few years later, an extraordinary artistic gift was developed inside of me and my paintings have been displayed in many different nations of the Earth.

The Sacrifice, Door of the Unusual

Many hours later we arrived at the Lobuche shelter. And right before us stood Nupste, one of the most amazing snow-covered peaks that make up part of base camp's amphitheater. Throughout this entire time we had not seen Everest.

We had climbed to five thousand meters, where the oxygen is scarce and our bodies quickly debilitate. The cabin we slept in did not have any dividers. It was deplorable, dirty and smelly. We had to sleep next to the Sherpas on top of boards, where pieces of dried yak dung were stored for fuel as it is highly flammable.

There were about twenty Sherpas from several expeditions laid down in front of the stove, taking up the entire floor. From the moment we arrived, we could hear rats squeaking beneath the boards, with the temperature quickly falling to ten degrees below zero.

The planks where we slept were arranged around a central heater that filled the room with smoke as it burned the dry manure. There was no water to wash the plates we ate on. They were cleaned with an old rag and that is how they served our food. We had no idea of what they were giving us to eat. But it was either that or nothing.

Gathered together with those Sherpas, in those harsh conditions, we decided to make the most of the situation and share the gospel with them. Only a few spoke a few words in English, most spoke Nepalese. So, we improvised a skit showing how God was made flesh to save humanity from its sins. Michael, an English Pastor from Gibraltar, acted out the representation of Jesus' sacrificed on the cross, while I played the role of a sinner giving my life for Him to save me.

The Sherpas carefully watched us as the Holy Spirit worked in their hearts. After we finished our improvised play, they all asked to receive Jesus in their heart. We were so moved and although the discomfort and pain in our bodies were almost unbearable, God's joy filled our hearts.

We arranged the sleeping bags so that the three women in our expedition were in the center, surrounded by our brothers, and devised a type of indoor tent with blankets to shelter ourselves for added protection. Altitude sickness struck some of our team members and they dozed off with terrible headaches.

We could hear them moaning throughout the night. The higher you are, the harder it is to sleep. Altitude produces intense insomnia, plus the cold, the stench and the sound of 30 snoring men piled up, one on top of the other, did not make it easy to rest. Rats ran underneath the laying boards so we had to close sleeping bags tight, so none of them would crawl in seeking a warm spot.

I could not fall asleep, and a sharp stomachache forced me to step outside the shelter. I asked Liliana to go with me.

The wind blew hard and low temperatures cut through our thick plume, insulated jackets right to our bones. The moon lit a few of the peaks that stood out between the clouds , which seemed to dance like ghosts around them. An infinite abandon-like solitude could be felt outside the shelter, as if Liliana and I were the only two people alive in that unending wasteland of rock and snow. We have entered the heights of what we called the shadow of death. The sensation was similar to the one on Mount Pisco in Peru, when Lencho suffered from his pulmonary edema.

My heart sank as I heard my teammates groaning from the altitude sickness. I recalled tormenting memories of Lencho's stifled breathing caused by the lack of oxygen in his blood.

After tonight, how many would continue? How many would want to turn back? And where would they turn back to? There was no medical help available until we reached Namche Bazaar that was still about five days journey.

This climb required years of physical and psychological training, as well as technical, high- mountaineering climbing knowledge. But the majority of the team did not even work out in a gym. They believed that their faith would take them as far as their physical abilities allowed. It was very difficult to rest that night . We slept about one or two hours. The guides suggested that if anyone did not feel well, they should remain one more day at the shelter and catch up with us later at base camp.

Greg, from the Wagner team, was not doing too well, but still decided to press on. The mountains do not tolerate errors, and to be honest, I though this was one of them.

The Sacrifice

That morning, while we ate breakfast, Rony shared that God had told him the devil's throne was not located on Everest's peak. He was very emphatic in saying that we needed to listen carefully about its location. Consequently, it was also necessary to lay down our summit attempt as a sacrifice on the altar. (Figuratively speaking)

It was a devastating blow for those of us who had trained and dreamt about that glorious moment for months. At the same time, we knew that the goal of conquering Everest was not for a human medal, but to tear down the throne we had been sent for. And... perhaps this saga would prove to be even more challenging, than making summit itself.

So with this in mind we started our daily trekking. Walking at five thousand meters above sea level is a very slow and strenuous process, requiring great physical exertion. We took this time of great concentration to realign our emotions. In order to reach our objective, we had to remain focused, and avoid opening any sentimental breaches that the enemy could use against us.

We arrived at the Gorak-shep refuge, the last one prior to base camp, completely exhausted. It was past five o'clock in the afternoon, and the only thing anyone could think of was getting a bite to eat and some rest. But that was not the case of Veronica or myself .

Oddly, we were both full of supernatural strength, as if we were just starting our trek of the day.

> When I clearly heard the Lord say,
> -"I want you and Veronica to climb the Kalapatar peak right now."

This was a mount that rose out of the Gorak-shep lakebed. It was about five thousand, seven hundred meters in altitude, which meant a three-hundred-meter climb from where we were located. It may not sound like much, but at that height, it would be the equivalent of climbing a hundred story building. And at that time of the day, it was definitely no easy task.

Rony, who was the spiritual authority of the group, agreed to our request and blessed our ascent.

The way we began our climb was unbelievable. We were practically running. We had a swift stride, to the point of arriving at the summit in little more than a half an hour later. It was absolutely miraculous.

Throughout the entire expedition up to that point, Everest was yet to be seen. It was past six in the afternoon and the sunset highlighted the white mountains with a vibrant orange color. The clouds literally danced with the summits, opening a few windows into the pinkish, blue sky.

On the Kalapatar summit, there was a rock in the shape of a stone bed. Had there been an ancient civilization there once, one could easily assume that this was their altar of sacrifices.

A strong and reverent presence could be felt. The voice of God told us to lay down on the rock. He asked us to surrender our ascent to the summit of the world on the altar as a sacrifice unto Him. Next to our own lives, it was the most precious offering we could give Him on that mount. We had to lay down every desire for human glory.

After all, that was exactly what every climber was after. It was what empowered the devil's throne, and granted him access to kill whomever he chose, since his wickedness required blood to continue surviving.

Tears streamed down our face as we silently worshipped our Heavenly Father and gave ourselves to Him with great love. We wanted His will to be done and not our own. In that moment, the clouds opened up and Everest's summit appeared before us as a luminous gold and fiery diamond, highlighted by the warm rays of the setting sun.

As we gazed at it for the first time, we started crying knowing that we would never be setting foot on its summit. We closed our eyes and laid our crown before God. Only Christ would get the glory, and no one else, for this was always our greatest satisfaction. Being reminded of this brought great joy, even more than reaching the top of the world.

The Holy Spirit then descended with great power engulfing us completely in Him. We ceased from feeling the heaviness of our own bodies, and started to feel weightless as if suspended inside a shining light. On the inside, I knew that the Lord was taking this expedition for Himself and that He would orchestrate everything else, so that He alone would sit on the heights of the world.

Suddenly we were no longer on that bed of stone. We do not know how much time went by, but a strong, cold breeze caused us to open our eyes. We experienced something that left us utterly speechless: we were standing on the

Everest summit. A golden sea of snowy peaks emerging from the clouds extended as far as the eye could see. No one had ever peered at what was before us, since no one had ever made summit at sunset. We looked at each another, unable to fully comprehend the wonder before us. We felt the snow and the rocks under our feet, but we could breathe freely without the need of oxygen tanks. I placed my arm around Veronica and gave our Heavenly Father all the glory. Our names would never be recorded in any Earthly chronicles, nor would we be tempted to glory in our own effort.

We never shared this with anyone, for it was a sublime and personal experience. And we also didn't want anyone to discredit what we had encountered. Furthermore, we didn't want anyone to take it the wrong way, or feel bad for not experiencing what we had. I kept it to myself for about seventeen years, until God gave me the freedom to share it in a book I wrote about the Spirit of Man,17 as well as now in this narrative.

17) The Spirit of Man, Ana Mendez Ferrell, Voice of the Light Editorial.

General in charge
takes the lead

We were approaching the end of what God had required of us, which was our courage, vigor and all-proof faith. Our limitation would soon turn into His unlimited power. From that moment on, He would take the lead, to introduce us into the most extraordinary dimension of the supernatural, we never dreamt it existed.

Visitors in the Death Zone

The Gorak Shep shelter was no better than the previous one. It was a shed that barely shielded us from the outside, where climbers, Sherpas, and rats all had to spend the night together.

Greg was still not doing too well, but he insisted on pressing on despite being advised the opposite by the guides. Two of our male climbers had remained behind in Lobuche trying to recover from altitude sickness.

It was about six in the morning, and the temperature had dropped to ten degrees below zero. The sun had not come out yet, and we could only see the first lights of dawn, when I suddenly made out what appeared to be the silhouettes of two men standing outside our shelter. Who were they? We never heard them arrive the night before. And...what were they doing outside in that bone-piercing cold? It was very odd indeed, because no one arrives at a shelter and remains outside, least of all at dawn.

The Sherpas had lit the fireplace in the center of the room and were making coffee for us. So, I decided to get out of my sleeping bag and greet the visitors.

The cold wind blew as I opened the door to invite them inside. They signaled back appreciating the gesture, but chose to remain outside. I noticed that they didn't have water bottles or backpacks. They wore pale blue insulated coats, with hoodies. I was intrigued, so I asked them what they were doing here.

"We are waiting for your group to walk with you to base camp," one of them said in English with a foreign accent. I offered them coffee as the temperatures were hovering around zero to which they replied that they were fine and for us to take our time that they would be waiting.

It took us about an hour to eat breakfast and pack our bags, while they waited.

When we came out, one of them led while the other covered the back. They didn't speak but rather skillfully navigated between the rocks of the moraine. We entered the Khumbu Glacier and the entire area was the valley of death consisting of huge rocks from landslides and crevasses. The route crossed over stretchs of glacier that appeared like a deep blue crystallized turquoise lake.

Walking through this area was very difficult because of the instability of the boulders. Most of the rocks required walking around but some of them required our balancing ourselves precariously as we shuffled over them. Death could be felt everywhere. The elaborate rock formations over the mountains seemed to come to life like enormous vultures watching our every step.

The water from the melting ice gushed furiously through countless canals, both on the surface and below, causing ghastly sounds that echoed through the rocky gorge of the moraine.

After walking for some time, we reached a narrow crossway that required our walking down into a deep abyss. Freezing rain began to fall making the rocks very slippery. Fear paralyzed Liliana as she began to cry terrified by the vertigo. Encouraging her did not help. I knew what she was feeling from my past experience of rappelling down vertical stonewalls during training.

Fear of heights was one of my greatest weaknesses. Nevertheless, I discovered the only way to overcome fears was to face every internal barrier that built them.

-"Don't look down," I said, while holding on to her arm.

-"Just think of the souls that will be delivered. They are the strength that drives us."

The visitor that was leading us stopped and walked up to Liliana. He didn't touch her but rather spoke to her in Spanish in a very calm manner. Then, out of nowhere, the leader of the Spanish expedition appeared together with another climber. They took hold of her and helped her find her courage and footing to proceed.

However, fear was spreading among the group. The team was faltering, and becoming more vulnerable by the minute. The wind became loud and threatening with its gusts sounds of terror. Nevertheless, the divine strength that lied within us encouraged us to press ahead. There was no turning back at this point.

As we entered the glacier, an enormous rectangular door of ice, appeared before us visible inside a deep ravine. It did not appear to be manmade nor did it look natural considering its shape and location. The inside was black, bottomless, and menacing. It looked to be hundred and twenty to hundred and fifty feet high and sixty feet wide.

During the times of intercession, the group had seen a door where the devil operated to a lost city under the ice castle. It was possible this was the entrance we had been searching for. Moreover, we had observed in the area one of the "holy men" or Chods. He was walking with a staff wearing a red turban and flower-beaded necklaces completely nude. He was a watchman, guarding the surrounding areas, where the door was located. We quietly passed by it, hoping to return later after we settled into base camp.

Suddenly an invisible power rose from the area attacking Rony and myself. It felt like a giant serpent had coiled around our bodies attempting to asphyxiate us. We were separated from the group and could only depend on the Holy Spirit to strengthen us to fight for one another lives. Every five to ten steps, it would attach it's self to us attempting to squeeze us to death. The battle was exhausting and lasted well over an hour. The enemy's goal was to destroy us.

As we approached our destination we recovered our breath and, overcame. The visitors were hidden from us for a time, but in the distance we could see them again. We arrived to what was called the ghost path; an endless procession of tall ice pinnacles that resembled Ku Klux Klan's hats, many were sixty to ninety feet high. There were thousands of them, sculpted throughout countless years by the sun and wind. We heard the various sounds created by the wind in such a way, that it seemed as if they were whispering to one another.

Our arrival to base camp had been a harrowing experience. There weren't many expeditions that year; only about five besides ours made up of two to six members each. There were about twenty small tents and three large ones in all. Our camp looked majestic right in the center. As I mentioned before, our Sherpas had gone ahead and set up the sleeping, dining, and kitchen tents.

The colorful flags we had given them served to decorate and set the limits for our mini- community of yellow tents. Like a Greek amphitheater, base camp was in the middle of a depression, surrounded by the walls of Everest, Lhotse, Nupste and Pumori's. It appeared like the bottom of an immense crown formed by the jagged mountain peaks. Ahead lie the impressive Icefall formed from large masses of broken ice, crevasses and seracs18 that measured ninety to hundred feet high.

Towards the top, Lhotses' white foothills hid the well-known village of Cwm (valley in Welsh), otherwise known as the Valley of Silence. In the distance, guarded by frozen protectors, and crystal ice scarf lie Everest. The summit was a fortress of untamed and invincible winds that screamed its dominance throughout the valley.

Everything was much higher and threatening than any photograph or film could ever capture. We felt insignificantly tiny in the middle of those monstrous rock and snow formations!

The tragedy from the previous year had caused a shortage of climbers during that season. This meant that amenities such as Internet, solar panel powered electric lighting; telephone center and showers were not available. Our only form of communication was radio and the only means of luxury was a shower that we used once during our entire stay. We stayed clean with wipes and heated wet towels from the camping stoves that were used to heat the tents.

Tents are pitched directly on the glacier at base camp. There was nothing level or flat on the ice, which meant the floors were anything but comfortable for sleeping or sitting. There are several dangers faced by those who set up on such unstable terrain. The first is that the glacier, which is in and of itself a frozen river, is constantly moving. The subterranean shifts can unexpectedly open up a crevasse between the tents swallowing them whole. It is estimated glaciers move ninety to one hundred and twenty centimeters per day.

Another danger is rock avalanches caused from strong winds that sound like a train station. Add that to the movement of the glacier and sleeping was a challenge to say the least. Although it might seem strange, the mountains themselves move. Everest moves four centimeters per year. For Asian scientists, the summit of the world is a good vantage point for the Eurasian and Indian tectonic plates, which clash in this highly seismic region. [19]

These movements within the Earth, no matter how small, could trigger great avalanches, which are responsible for most deaths among climbers.

---

18) Gigantic ice formations which form when the ice is shaken after the glacier moves and crevices open up on it. 19) http://www.prensalibre.com/internacional/terremoto-de-nepal-desplazo-40-centimetros-el-monte-everest

We would soon deem staying in those smelly, rustic mountain lodges of the past 11 days, a paradise, compared to what awaited us. The only advantage would be breathing fresh air, since it was impossible to do so in the smoke-filled shelters of burning yak dung.

Completely exhausted, we had used our last ounce of strength to place our bags in our tents and reach the dining tent.

Our blue-coated visitors waited outside to welcome us. They had not stopped to eat or drink at all, so I invited them to stay and eat dinner with us.

-"Where will you be staying?" I asked. "Would you like to join us for dinner?" I was astonished by their reply.

-"No, thank you. We will be heading back tonight. We won't be staying here." "What? But it's nighttime. You cannot possibly return now, it is too dangerous."

-"Don't worry. We know well our way back."

-"Well, then please at least eat something before you go," I insisted.

-"No, thank you very much. We are fine."

This was not normal. Who were they?

---

20 Shalom means peace in Hebrew.

-"Where are you from?" I inquired, full of curiosity.

They stopped before replying and said,
-"From Israel. We are Israelites."

I got very excited and told them we had been sent by the God of Israel to consecrate the heights of the Earth to the Eternal Father.

They smiled joyfully, but somehow by the look in their eyes, we could tell they already knew. They waited for the last member of our team to arrive and bid their farewell with a "Shalom,"20. They never ate nor drank anything and no climber that ever makes it to base camp turns back at night. That is when we realized that they had to be angels sent by God for that particularly difficult section of the mountain.

We often discussed and asked ourselves why we would sometimes see them walking among us and then simply disappear along paths where it should have been easy to see them at a distance. There was always a hint of mystery in this part of the trek.

It was obvious that something was happening in the mountains. Grotesque clouds surrounded the peaks as terrifying countenances emerged from the rock formations, together with lights that descended like pink vapors shrouding them. There was much more spiritual activity taking place than we could have ever imagined.

a Death Encounter

The visitors had just left, when Greg's condition took a turn for the worse. He felt like his head was exploding and I knew it was brain edema. A lack of air pressure at around five thousand six hundred meters above sea level can sometimes cause body fluids to fill the brain or the lungs. And if not treated immediately, it can result in chronic consequences or even death.

I approached the Spanish expedition, whom we had met previously in various teahouses. One of them was a doctor and they were equipped to deal with an emergency.

The doctor and another one of the Spaniards quickly arrived at the dining tent to examine Greg. "This is a case of advanced edema. We must place him inside a hyperbaric chamber. Do you have any oxygen with you?"

-"Yes, we have seventy tanks we had planned to use for the summit climb."

-"Bring some quickly." He exclaimed, aware of the severity of the situation.

They brought the chamber from their camp. It was a restricted, red-plastic cylinder made to fit only one person with a transparent, rubber window in front of the person's face. The idea was to inject oxygen with sufficient pressure to simulate a lower altitude of two thousand meters, causing the liquid accumulated in the person's brain to flow back to his organs so the body can eliminate it.

Greg's face had turned purple and his breathing had slowed down greatly. Death could be felt all around. His eyes began to pop out as he gestured the intense pain he felt.

-"How serious is his condition?" I asked.

-"We will know in a few hours. It is crucial that he doesn't lose consciousness."

As exhausted as we were, we took turns praying for our friend, who spent the next sixteen hours inside the claustrophobic container that nearly exploded from the pressure. That evening we felt some relief in the midst of those terrible moments when our other two members of the team, who had fallen behind in Lobuche, finally arrived to base camp.

The night was intense. The battle against death oppressed us all. We were in the middle of the highest cemetery in the world and could still sense the ridden of the 1996 expedition striving to survive. Darkness, fear and a feeling of insignificance and inexperience make you question everything, yet this is the greatest battle you must overcome.

If fire were to symbolize the highest expression of life, then ice can easily symbolize death.

Liliana and I were not feeling too good either. Our headaches were so unbearable that I had to lie down. My heart had made an extraordinary effort, and I could barely catch my breath. I prayed in that tent asking that I would not get as bad as Greg since there was only one hyperbaric chamber. Had I or someone else on the team needed it, it would have resulted in a dire tragedy.

The night seemed endless. The wind shook the tents vigorously. A strong snowstorm hit base camp, dipping the temperature to minus twenty degrees Celsius. The tents were slowly buried under a thick blanket of snow.

The Gentle Voice after the Storm

The morning light lit up the inside of my small yellow tent. I started to stretch inside my sleeping bag to loosen my stiff muscles, and as I did, a coat of ice fell right on my face. I was now wide-awake. The ice had been formed by the vapor from breathing. The breath freezes at such low temperatures and then detaches from the inside of the tent whenever there is movement.

Little by little, everyone made their way out of their tents and headed towards the dining tent. Greg was now doing much better, and everyone was happy to see him outside of the chamber having breakfast and talking.

Having been so close to death and feeling so frail after that terrible night had made us all more sensitive than usual.

The Spirit of intercession fell on us and we began to pray spontaneously. Genuine heartfelt tears were shed, crying for the nations in captivity. We prayed that His light would shine on them to receive the gospel.

We carried tiny flags of the nations, as well as small symbolic objects that most people would probably laugh at. It wasn't the power of those material objects, like a Bible or dagger, that would make the difference, but it was the Eternal God of Glory anointing His children in order for Him to manifest. It is not what we do prophetically, is who we are, and the level of His Light that we carry that makes the difference.

Gradually we realized that our tears were not our own, but they were God's embracing the nations that were enslaved by such darkness.

The room started to fill with the presence of God, and we were immersed in the weight of His glory to the point that we could no longer move.

-"I see the heavens open," marveled Rony, as we all felt the bliss that captivated him. "I can see the mounts of Everest, Nuptse and Lohtse forming a seat or a throne. I also see a majestic and spectacular figure descending upon Everest's peak. His face is a shining light, but I can't distinguish his features. As He sits with great authority upon the throne, I see the mountains melt before him and crushed beneath his feet. He then speaks in a loud voice and says,

-"The Great Babylon has fallen! And He says again,

-"The Great Babylon has fallen! "He adds: Don't hold back, but shout it in the mountains and on the roof tops everywhere that Babylon has fallen."

It was Jesus Christ Himself manifesting in the vision.

The faces of millions of people trapped in their slave-like destinies trapped in regions of terrible darkness began to appear before our spiritual eyes. They were groaning in the midst of terrible pain, despair and devastation.

-"Oh Father, how you long to have them face-to-face in your glorious freedom!" exclaimed Rick. "Anoint us as your servants and as the servants of these people whom you love so dearly."

Greg, voice cracking, began to paraphrase one of the prophecies given to Isaiah the prophet,

-"These are your instruments that come from the ends of the Earth. They have been willing to train for months at a time and lay down their lives to advance Your Kingdom as it is written in your word. They are your devoted ones, who rejoice in Your glory. They are your brave ones who have come to declare the thunder of Your justice upon the mountains."

They were great solemn moments of humbling ourselves before God, and understanding that everything depended on Him and Him alone. We were instruments completely submitted to His hands. If the mountain was not forgiving with mistakes, much less were the devil and his hosts.

After praying and thanking God for all of us being alive, we bid farewell to Greg and Rick. The doctor told us tit was not a good idea for him to remain at that high altitude. Rick decided to sacrifice his expedition to go down with him. It was very sad to watch them leave.

By that time, the rest of the Americans, including Doris and her intercessors, had made it to the Everest View Hotel. Somehow, she had bypassed Santa Subba's threats and set him in his place. And our team members would now join them in the rear guard.

Night fell, and with it the temperature as well. The only camp with kerosene-based heating was our dining tent. So, all the climbers from the other expeditions came to warm themselves up and strike a friendship with us. There were two Spanish teams, another team with two French climbers, another with two Italian c and finally a group of Koreans that never got very close to us.

It was wonderful to have fellowship with them. Each night they would bring us something from their countries. The French would bring cheese, the Italians expresso and the Spaniards cold meats. We shared meals with them and had long talks about God and the unique mysteries tucked away in the mountains. They shared about their adventures and the complications that can develop high up on the mountain. Indeed, it was quite insightful for our group of novices.

None of them were part of a commercial expedition, but

rather were simple men, philanthropists, nature lovers and fans of extreme sports.

We all agreed that a mountain experience should be special. It should lift the spirit and lead to knowing God and oneself even more.

The smaller and weaker a person is in any given circumstance, the greater the possibility of encountering their Creator and understanding their destiny. This was the role that these large mountains played, reminding us of how small we were and how great the One who created it all is.

Approaching these large formations of snow and rock demanded our utmost respect. This was their territory, not ours. Breaking the rules meant suffering great losses, and even our own lives. They are the likes of majestic hierarchs who select their most intimate friends. They are the ones who choose which way to access their most prized and secret places of their icy kingdoms. Not just anyone can get there, but only those who are allowed in, when they long for it with all their strength.

This is how they can be likened to God who sits on Mount Zion. Moreover, it is also here that the audacity of walking arrogantly can easily lead to a person's demise as well. However, those who search with all their heart and lay down everything to have Him (God) are taken up to His high places where He sets them there with Him. Everyone can reach God's foothills, but not everyone can reach His summits.

Mountains hold a very special place in God's wisdom and strategies. They are a symbol of government and authority, which is why the devil, has always coveted them. Every time God did something that changed the history, which He Himself penned, it always involved a mountain and a man connected to it.

God saved Noah, who then in turn consecrated the Earth on Mount Ararat. Abraham became the father of nations when he was led to sacrifice his son, Isaac, on Mount Moriah. Moses received the tables of the law on Mount Sinai. Elijah defeated the priests of Baal on Mount Carmel, and Jesus gave His life on Mount Calvary.

The Dragon's Throat

and the door of the underworld

The following morning we all felt our strength replenished. The sun shone upon the white, snow-covered tents that began to melt, revealing the valley of small, golden domes at base camp.

We gathered together to pray that morning and seek divine direction. Rony told me about a dream from God, which was also the essence of what led him to be part of this expedition. He took a piece of paper out of his backpack where he had written the dream down and read it to all us.

-"I was transported to a place surrounded by high mountains," he began to share.

-"And I knew that it was Everest and the surrounding summits. I saw a dragon with seven heads, but its strength was in the neck. There was a horrible woman ridding the dragon, like the harlot in Revelation cursing the nations. Then, I was given a sword from heaven and I saw myself plunging it into the dragon's neck until it fell dead."

Then he added,
-"The day we were climbing towards base camp, and we passed by that dark door, I felt that the dragon was aware of our arrival and was trying to slay us. That is precisely where its neck is located, and that is where we need to go."

-"As a matter of fact," I added, "the inside of the door was in the shape of a throat."

The Throat

We decided to set out towards that place. There was a sense of unrest in the atmosphere. We could not see it, but we knew that the dragon was restless and fearful, like an animal aware that danger was quickly approaching. There was an invisible light that surrounded us, like a mantle placed upon us to hide us from the dragon's sight. It was the blood of Jesus awakening us.

Crows flew around in a frenzy attempting to obstruct our hike.

But faith moved us forward. We were not going in our own strength, but in God's. We approached the site where the door was located. It was difficult to avoid reminiscing the deadly attack we had just encountered two days earlier, but we could not allow a single thought to frighten us. While it is true that our battle was in the spiritual realm, we were also aware that powers of darkness use the forces of nature to manifest in the physical realm.

We started to hear a roar of strong winds and tumbling rocks. The clouds moved swiftly, like a stampede seeking to hide among the cliffs or attempting to run away.

One could hear rumbling in the mountains. An angelic presence could be felt everywhere. We knew that Michael the Archangel and his angels had come down to wage this battle against the dragon and its hosts. Our voices thundered with great power, activating and mobilizing the hosts of heaven. Some read the fall of Babylon, described in the Bible, at the top of their lungs. Rony engaged in a great battle, prophesying against the dragon he had seen in his dream that was now squirming and twisting around the hills and the ghost valley.

Mariano, a prayer warrior of our team and I, carefully approached the door. The ground was slippery and unsafe. There were enormous rocks on top of the threshold threatening to fall at the slightest movement of the glacier. An infernal breeze arose out of there, similar to the one I had felt in a cave in Catemaco, the city of witches in Mexico. I had seen the eyes of satan there, yellow, filled with hatred and rage, menacing like a huge male goat.

I glanced inside, and it was literally like looking down a giant, icy bottomless throat. We were standing on loose rocks that could barely remain on the cavern's frozen ledge. The strength that empowered the great harlot, the mother of the abominations of the Earth who blasphemously took on the title of the queen of heaven, rose from that spot.

Suddenly, the throat became alive before me. A vibration emitted from the bottom of it causing the walls of ice to take on the liquid reflection of a mirage. For a moment, I was able to see the spiritual reality that unfolded before me. I could hear the sound of a grim and hypnotic voice emanating from within. It would transform into a dark substance, extending like a layer of darkness from the mountain towards all the nations of the Earth. One couldn't imagine the magnitude, but it imprisoned the minds of millions of people, blinding them keeping them enslaved to idolatrous systems and making them believe all types of false religious systems, regardless of how ludicrous they were to human reasoning. Countless masses of people yielded to them as unconditional, superstitious minions, subjugated by the fear of death, pain, and unspeakable horrors.

I fell to my knees, humbling myself before God for the millions of people who succumb to the great harlot and her system of captivity. I wept for them and cried out for their deliverance. Afterwards, imbued with the indignation generated within in me, I took a Bible and a stone, placed them in a bag, and threw it inside the throat with all my strength.

-"I come in the name of Jesus Christ against your deceiving power, your spellbinding voice, and your lies!" I yelled out. "And I declare that from this moment forward, the voice of God and His word shall be heard by every person in captivity. Let the voice of the Almighty ring out, and His angels resonate from this place!"

The Bible began to sink as the throat's icy, narrow walls began to tumble. I saw it like a sharp sword piercing through the dragon's neck.

Then Rony took the sword that was assigned to him by the Spirit of God and lunged it into the dragon's neck at the top part of the cave.

The dragon breathed his last breath, roaring in the wind that quickly intensified. The clouds began to close in and turn dark. Each time we struck a blow the sky would manifest with raging storms, which can turn especially severe at those high altitudes. Danger was eminent, so we quickly made our way back to base camp.

As night fell, the mountains took on the form of dark, eerie faces that lurked around us. However, God kept us in perfect peace. The prayers in which we persevered formed a dome-like protection that made us invisible to the enemy, allowing us to proceed with the prophetic strategies God instructed us to carry out.

Death continued to stalk us at every turn and desperation began to settle into several members of the team. The uncertain circumstances we faced had started to take a toll on some of our teammates. The physical strain caused by poor sleep, temperatures of under twenty degrees Celsius.

Not only that, but one of the climbers on the verge of death from the Korean expedition had to be evacuated by helicopter. Seeing the body of an experienced climber in that condition made the risks we were facing even more real. It felt like a bucket of cold water on those who were already reaching their limits.

These circumstances gave way to great tension. Rony decided that his mission was over and that he needed to go down. The rest of the team debated between returning or moving forward. Liliana and myself along with other teammates felt that the mission was still not complete. But since Rony was our spiritual authority, his decision was causing great disaccord.

Rony and I went away to pray, as did the rest of the team. After seeking God's direction for some time, Rony turned to me and said,

-"I am going back down, but I will continue covering you in prayer. It is important that you do what you must do. If I stay, I'll probably stand in the way of what God wants to do through you and you need to move freely with those who are willing to continue."

On the one hand, I felt real sad that he was leaving. He was, after all, my spiritual authority and dear friend, but on the other hand, I also knew I had an assignment to fulfill.

Eduardo, his trainer, and Mariano from Mexico joined Rony. They hiked down to the Everest View Hotel in Shiangboche where they continued to intercede for those of us who would remain.

The team was cut down to six, three of which had never climbed a mountain before nor seen a crampon or an ice axe. These were Michael, the Englishman, Tato the Spaniard and Liliana from Columbia. The rest of the team was Vero and Lencho, my beloved disciples, and I.

In the high mountains, it is hard to see a team breaking up. To see all those who suffered with you and believed with all their heart that the mission could be accomplished, now leaving the camp.

However, everyone has their own mission and strength, and they are all worthy of our honor and respect.

One thing that I've learned climbing mountains for God is that reaching a goal or making the summit means the entire team also makes it as well, because we are all one body.

While Rony, and the two other teammates left base camp the following morning, we were determined to seek God for the following steps that we needed to take.

That day was a great blessing indeed, for it was the day we got to take a shower. The Sherpa emptied their dining tent and melted ice so that we could have several buckets of hot water to bathe and wash our hair.

After so many days of making it on wet wipes and small pots of hot water on our bodies, the idea of an entire bucket of boiling water was itself like paradise.

We each took turns, and I cannot even begin to describe how those cups of hot water running down my head and shampoo washing my stiff hair felt after so many days of sweat and grit. There are many things we take for granted in civilization, but which deep down we should really be grateful for such as the thousands of years the world did without technology and urban advancements that we can now enjoy.

Everest

Part 3

The Heart of the Mountain

The crown formed by the high summits at base camp, the glacier and every other peak, formed a complex structure in the spiritual realm, harboring the headquarters of the falsely proclaimed queen of heaven. It was almost as if the entire site was alive, and as such, it had a heart. And it was located right at the base of the Icefall. It was a very dark place, spiritually speaking. The waters that irrigated Tibet and Nepal and fed its sacred rivers flowed from there. It was like a well out of which demons arose to slay those whom Sagarmatha asked for as a sacrifice.

We spent hours worshipping God in that spot until we felt that the blood of Jesus had descended to purge that tributary, so the waters from heaven would now flow from that site.

As days went by, the location of the devil's throne became even clearer. It was above the Icefall, near camp one, about 6000 meters above sea level.

During our stay at base camp, we had carved the names of God everywhere on the ice, decreeing that the heights of the Earth belonged to Him. We had delimited the territory with symbols alluding to His presence and His covenant with man. We had fixed powerful decrees taken from God's Word and established an altar made up of twelve stones for His glory. Many times, we saw angels ascend and descend with our natural eyes, positioning themselves for something great that was about to take place.

While the storms intensified at base camp, fog covered the rear guard's camp in Shiangboche. However, they continued to intercede outdoors despite the winds and intense cold, reading scripture out loud and saturating the mountains with God's living Word.

It was about seven o'clock in the morning on September 22nd, when I unzipped my tent to step out. As I looked outside, the glory of God filled me. I could hardly speak. There was something very special, intangible, but magnificent at the same time. I summoned everyone else with reverence. My spirit was compelled to worship in the tongues of the Holy Spirit.

There were hundreds of angels that had assembled together on all the peaks. A light-filled mist overshadowed the rock pinnacles that stood out from the slopes, resembling dozens of temples piercing through the clouds. It was as if the collected abominations of thousands of years were being presented before God in heaven itself.

The light in the heights of the Lohtse peak seemed to form luminescent swords that were reflected on the other summits. An odd radiance, visible to our eyes, began to emerge from Everest's northern face, like a living fire arriving to crown the mountain. It was as intense as the sun, albeit coming from the North, not the East.

The radiance continued to grow giving way to a strange phenomenon: between the light and the rocky pyramid that makes up Everest's peak, a black mountain began to take form. It was a giant shadow, as if the spiritual mountain was being exposed so everyone could see it. The shadows, however, were not being projected from the mountain, but they came behind it, between the light and the boulder. This is physically impossible. It was as if an eclipse was being produced by something intangible that lay behind the mountain.

We were speechless and ecstatic. I had the video camera in my hands, and as my spirit exploded into worship, I began to film everything just as it happened.

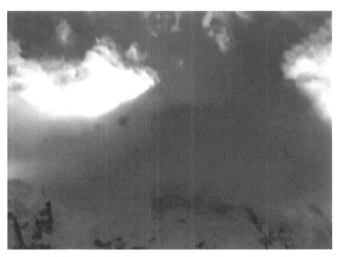

Mount of Darkness, just as it was filmed

The clouds intensely glowing were filled with angels that fought and judged the mountain of darkness of the queen of heaven. We had never seen anything like it before. It was clearly the spiritual world manifesting in the natural one.

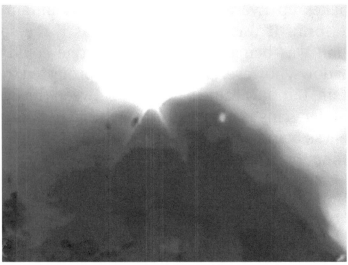

Light from the northern part of the darkness

The glory of God filled it all, and we could hardly remain on our feet. We wept with gratitude and brokenness at the sight of being exposed to such magnificence. It was as if God himself was taking His seat on the heights of the Earth to conquer and rule it.

An eagle formed in the sky. God himself was fashioning the battle before our very eyes.

Radiance crowned the summit of the world and two visible swords of light emerged out of it splitting the spiritual mount.

Eagle as it was filmed

I could not continue filming. Together with everyone else, I fell to the ground giving glory to the Maker and Lord of the heavens and the Earth. God was taking his seat on the throne of the top of the world!

And His voice could be heard as clear as crystal,

-"Today you shall climb to the throne in the harlot's den. Only six of you will go up, my children. You will not take guides, or carriers or oxygen tanks. You will not climb through the fixed- route set for the other climbers, but I will lead you through a different one. My spirit will be your guide and my angels will keep you from the icefall's slides and crevasses. And I will be your strength and your oxygen," says the Lord.

We felt an amazing anointing coming upon us, invigorating us with the power and the ability to climb. It felt as if we had become climbers with years of experience, filled with a large amount of high-mountaineering knowledge.

What had just taken place in the spirit must be established in the natural, just as Jesus said, "I don't do anything, that I don't see the Father doing." Whatever the Father did in the heavens, Jesus would reproduce it on Earth. And He was sending us the same way. We must not do or say anything that we first do not see the Father doing or saying, or as is more commonly known in the Lord's Prayer, "Let it be done on Earth as it is in heaven."

In the midst of that sublime atmosphere that filled us all, we set off towards the great battle against the throne of Babylon and the queen of heaven.

Climbing the Icefall at Everest, without a guide or outside

the regular fixed route and ladders, was suicide in the eyes of any climber. This was the site on the southeast route most feared by experts about 6000 meters above sea level. It is there the glacier moves abruptly and splits due to the slope's incline. Technically speaking, it was the most complicated stretch of an expedition to the summit of the world, and the place where most people loose their lives.

As the glacier slides internally because of the rugged terrain, the giant ice mass breaks up into large, unsteady blocks known as seracs. Some as large as a twelve story building which can crumble at any time, making it like playing Russian roulette for any climber. Furthermore, due to the constant shift in the region, huge ice crevasses are formed anywhere from twenty to twenty-five meters wide and thirty to one hundred meters deep. Normally, ladders and static ropes are used to cross them with extreme care.

The Icefall

Icefall Crevasses

The other issue is that there are several invisible crevasses, as the ice closes in the surface, forming a thin crystal layer that conceals them. And when it snows, covers it further appearing like a solid surface. It takes much experience to recognize them and know how to test the ground that you step on.

Ice was a new experience for the three of us who had semi-prepared for it. These types of glaciers do not exist in Mexico. We had to train for it by watching a video called Learn how to climb on ice.

Ana, Michael & Vero Checking A Crevasse

So, this is what the team assigned with the task of defeating this monster consisted of: six inexperienced climbers that had watched a video but trusted God and His angels would lead and protect them every step of the way.

Convinced by the supernatural faith of the One who had sent us, we made our way towards the Icefall. We entered in through a region distant from the government checkpoint, which checks for government permits.

Since we did not have any ropes or ladders, we had to cross the crevasses, by either jumping over the narrowest parts or rappelling down with ropes and then climbing up the crevasse walls with ice axes. The video we had seen clearly demonstrated how to place the tip of the crampons on the ice and pull ourselves up using the ice axes.

At any given moment, we would come across the bones of frozen cadavers buried by the Glacier's movements. As the ice shifted or melted, the bodies of the unfortunate mountaineers were exposed.

Lencho, Vero and I had trained for this moment psychologically, since we knew that we would come across the deceased, but the others, however, were not prepared for it.

Fear gripped Liliana and Michael, who stopped when they saw them. They were overwhelmed, trying to recover their nerve as best they could. Michael pulled a picture of his children out of his down jacket and pressed it against his chest. He shed a tear and as every good Englishman, wiped it away immediately and mustered his courage to press on.

The ice castle we were headed to could now be made out in the distance. A figure of a virgin naturally sculpted out of an enormous rock, stood out among the ice peeks.

Our Team ascending the Icefall

We were closely approaching our goal, when we suddenly heard a jarring noise, like the sound of dozens of locomotives pulling out at the same time.

A giant avalanche quickly descended from Everest's heights. It felt like half of the mountain was coming apart and heading our way.

The cloud formed by millions of tiny crystals released by the massive avalanche quickly engulfed us. We recalled the conversations we had had with our friends from the Spanish expedition. They had told us about how breathing in the cloud that forms around an avalanche is extremely dangerous. Inhaling those tiny ice needles in the cloud could quickly lead to respiratory failure.

We yelled out from diverse points, "Cover yourselves!" hoping to be heard in the midst of that terrifying rumble, as we were about sixty to ninety feet apart from one another.

The icy cloud covered us while tons of ice quickly following, aiming to take our lives out. Each of us began to pray intensively not knowing at what moment we would all be buried alive.

It was like being in the middle of an Earthquake with everything around you falling, and all you see is the inside of your windbreaker struck by a sand storm made up of millions of crystals. Ice could be heard breaking and falling apart on every side. There was no doubt that dozens of large seracs were tumbling down. Every second felt like an eternity. We were believing that God's hand would keep us...but...

-"Where were my teammates? I asked myself. "Were they all still alive? When would I be buried? Would I have the strength to break through the ice when it falls on me? How would God deliver us? Or was He asking for our lives in exchange for the deliverance of the 10/40 window?"

It was clearly none other than that abominable "mother goddess," who was violently revolting, like a wounded beast, against the Almighty, and we were right smack in the middle of that devastating attack.

All I could think about while I was still under that thick fog of ice was my children waving goodbye and embracing me amidst tears saying, "Please come back, Mommy!"

Then suddenly a loud cracking noise of ice breaking was heard. The glacier was opening up. It was a harrowing blare with everything shaking beneath our feet.

Suddenly everything stopped, and there was complete silence. The ice needles from the cloud stopped clashing against my windbreaker, as I carefully cleared my face, and the high pinnacles began to slowly reappear in the midst of the ice fog that dissipated.

I was able to see Liliana and Tato, but I couldn't see anyone else.

-"Are you alright?" I cried out.

-"Yes...yes, everything is ok," they all answered with a shivering voice. "Vero? Lencho? Michael?" We yelled, fearing the worse.

After an intense, stress-filled moment, Vero appeared and then Michael, but Lencho was nowhere to be seen.

We kept yelling, but there was no response. We went back to look for him, since he was our rear guard.

We saw an arm sticking out under a huge block of ice, then another. Vero ran towards him. And there he was, shaking off the snow, a bit dazed but with a great smile when he saw his sister. They embraced each other tightly. It was an emotional moment for us all, reminding us of how frail our lives are in the face of catastrophes of this magnitude. "Without God we are nobody and we can't do anything," were the conclusions uttered while still shaking, crying and hugging each other. These were very touching moments indeed.

Once the cloud had settled, we were amazed at seeing the unbelievable miracle the hand of God had just wrought before us. Just a few feet away, an enormous crack had opened up and swallowed the entire avalanche.

We were both stunned and amazed, not knowing how to react in the face of such indescribable greatness. Our emotions ranged from terror to gratitude, to gratefulness, to faith and to the boldness we needed to continue, since we were yet to reach our goal.

No one could give up now. We had to remain united at

all costs. We had to minister to Liliana and Michael who were still shaken, holding pictures of their children that they always carried with them.

-"Don't fear beloved," I told them. "If God did not allow us to perish in this avalanche, it is because He is in control of everything and we're going to make it back safe and sound victoriously."

After a few moments, one by one, they began to wipe their tears away and lift their countenance to heaven agreeing to move forward.

The avalanche had changed the landscape considerably. We would have to find another route to the ice castle, amidst the seracs.

We were still about nine hundred linear feet away, standing on uneven ground. The oppression was strong. One could sense evil spirits in the spirit stalking us among the jagged ice formations. Their grotesque and demonic faces seemed to emanate from everywhere.

We felt like we had just entered a haunted house, with the possibility of a hideous apparition materializing out of nowhere. There was death imprinted in every ice formation.

I tried to film while narrating what we were experiencing,

but the magnetism produced by the darkness erased the images on my camera, only leaving noisy static on the screen.

We walked, carefully testing the ice, making sure it was solid before stepping on it.

The stress gradually increased. Our hearts pounded rapidly despite the high altitude, where a heart tends to beat more slowly. At that height, one breathes much more slowly, making it difficult to speak. The lack of oxygen plus the oppression in that place made the little air left hard to breath. It feels like one is carrying sixty pounds on the back.

We finally arrived at the high ice wall that protected the castle of the queen of heaven. It was very similar to the one I had seen in my dreams, but much more ominous. The only way to break into it would be by skillfully climbing it. Lencho went up with a rope first to tie them one by one and hoist them up. It was about at least a fifty feet high, surrounded by a very deep chasm that made it even more perilous. The crystalized, icy crevasses that sank in the unfathomable bottomless darkness caused us to tremble with fear. We could feel a force pulling us into the precipice. The voices of the enemy could be heard mocking us and urging us to throw ourselves into the dark hole of the icy cliffs.

Ana scaling an icy wall prior to arriving at our destination

Once Lencho found a rock to tie the rope on, he tossed it over the ledge so we could start climbing. Vero was the first to go up, so she could help from the top. Then I tied Liliana by the waist and pulled her up half way with everyone's help. Then Lencho and Vero finished helping her get to the top by hoisting her up the rest of the way. Anguish groans could be heard coming out of her, considering the imminent danger she was facing, as her soul screeched in terror. One by one we made our way up trying to avoid looking down. We had to overcome. There was no possibility of turning back at that point.

The vertigo caused by our inexperience and fear of heights caused many to break down into tears upon reaching the top. We encouraged each another as we raised our sight to the enormous rock formation that ruled the throne of darkness.

We were so small, like a tourist standing at the base of the statue of liberty in New York.

Ana & Michael writing decrees on the great
boulder that symbolized the "great harlot"

It was hard to approach her as a magnetic-type of discharge repulsed us. I finally placed my hand on it and wrote the decrees of her downfall on the rock, clearly feeling God's hand crushing and sinking her.

Symbolically we disconnected the crown of England from that site, as well as every nation that had ever been consecrated to that throne.

The anointing became stronger, and to our surprise, we heard ourselves screaming at the top of our lungs, as if we were at sea level.

We decreed the prophecy outlined in the book of Jeremiah, announcing the fall of Babylon and of the idols that sustain it:

*Declare among the nations, proclaim,
and set up a standard;
Proclaim—do not conceal it—Say, 'Babylon is taken, Bel is shamed. Merodach is broken in pieces; her idols are humiliated; her images are broken in pieces.*

I have laid a snare for you; you have indeed been trapped, O Babylon, and you were not aware; you have been found and also caught, because you have contended against the Lord.

The Lord has opened His armory and has brought out the weapons of His indignation; for this is the work of the Lord God of hosts.

A sword is against the soothsayers, and they will be fools. A sword is against her mighty men, and they will be dismayed.

A drought is against her waters, and they will be dried up. For it is the land of carved images, and they are insane with their idols.

At the noise of the taking of Babylon the Earth trembles, And the cry is heard among the nations.

Though Babylon were to mount up to heaven, And though she were to fortify the height of her strength, Yet from Me plunderers would come to her," says the Lord.[21]

21) Note: Jeremiah 50 and 51 was read in its entirety, but I only used a few extracts in this book.

After proclaiming all the decrees God had given us, the atmosphere began to change. The power of God could be felt strongly as we performed several symbolic acts representing the structure's downfall.

We proceeded to build an altar unto God placing a Torah22, wine, bread and a rod at the same location as the throne. These items symbolized the ones found in the Ark of the Covenant, which were the Tables of the Law, mana and Aaron's rod that budded.

Furthermore, planting a flag is an undeniable sign that an army has dethroned an enemy kingdom to establish the kingdom they represent.

This is the moment I had dreamt of and longed for with all my heart. It is the most glorious instant of any battle and the defining moment of any victory. This is the point where history is made, ushering forth the light of change. For months, I imagined what Armstrong must have felt when he planted that flag on the moon. And as we pondered that unique moment, we designed a beautiful flag with all the names of God from the Bible. It was red as the blood of Jesus with gold letters, trimmed with beautiful golden brocade. I took it in my hands trying to prolong this fulfilling moment in my life. We all held hands, since it was not just one person who was conquering this throne but one entire united body: The body of Christ. Holding it tightly in my free hand like a large sword that was about to pierce through the bowels of hell, I pitched it in the snow and raised my voice with great authority crying out,

22) The Old Testament written on a scroll in Hebrew

"The roof of the world now belongs to Jesus Christ!"

What God Himself had done in the spirit that same morning, we were now reenacting in the natural realm, in the exact place indicated by Him to establish His flag and His name.

It was truly an exciting moment, one we had experienced over-and-over again in our imagination, but that now was a reality.

Planting the flag of God Almighty on the Roof of the World

While still holding hands, we all cried out seven times in one accord, "Shaback!" which was the term the Israelite army yelled when the walls of Jericho came tumbling down to take the Promise Land.

It is a word that expresses the highest amount of glory possible to God after battle.

We were still celebrating and embracing one another, when the voice of God came to me and almost audibly said,

> -"Quickly rush down and leave base camp no later than eleven o'clock in the morning because I am going to destroy it all."

Lencho playing the Shofar as a sign of victory

It was already late in the afternoon and swiftly returning to base camp was almost an impossible feat. Bear in mind that it had taken us almost an entire day to reach that site. We recalled the humorous Spaniards who shared how they sometimes slid down the mountain as if it were a giant slide.

We looked at each other and nodded in agreement, "Why not try it?"

After fending off the great wall, we would have to find the right slopes to slide down using our ice axes to keep us from falling off a precipice or crevasse. During some of our training climbs, we had had to use this method for emergency descents; and though it required some knowledge, it wasn't really that complicated. So, Lencho, Vero and I would jump first, and form a barrier at the end of the slope to stop the others from falling into a crevice. It was important to know how to hammer our ice axes down in the snow to be able to stop, and then help stop the others with our bodies to avoid taking any chances.

The sliding and crashing into one another, and the screaming on the way down caused great laughter and fun in the process.

And so, after sliding and climbing down the crevices, we finally arrived at base camp around eight at night.

As we slid and laughed our way down, I couldn't help but think how we were going to leave base camp by eleven in the morning.

Taking everything down and mounting it on yaks was an impossible task.

It took up to sixty pack animals to take everything up there. And once the beasts are unloaded, they just return to their owners. Getting that many animals together requires a team of Sherpas going through every town and hamlet in the mountain, asking shepherds for one or two animals to rent, if they have any available. This task would take days to coordinate.

On the other hand, Santa Subba, who had disappeared completely, was not a viable option either.

Therefore, the only solution was to lose it all and leave early the next morning with just our backpacks.

That evening, we were able to speak with Rony and Doris by radio and share everything that had happened and how God had manifested.

We were ecstatic, celebrating in the dining tent, when I stepped out to get something from my tent. It was a clear night, and the moon had just begun to wane, so not too many stars were visible.

I was walking with my lantern when I heard a noise like horse hooves coming from heaven. I looked up to see what it was, and just as clear as one would see something here on the Earth, I saw a white horse with Michael, the archangel, mounted on it.

Both he and the horse shone as if their bodies were made of millions of diamonds. His silver cape waved in the air, releasing flashes of light. The horse bucked and moved its head around as if ready to take off.

I was shaking, and my eyes teared up as I peered at the vision.

-"We are all here," he uttered in a commanding voice with great authority, as he turned around to look at me.

In that instant, the sky was filled with stars, as I had never seen before in my life, even on the highest mountain with the clearest sky. Then both horse and jockey dissolved into the stars.

I was stunned in excitement. My heart felt like it was about to burst with joy. The greatness of God and His way of doing things has always led me to a place of deep humility and of recognizing how infinitely small and unworthy we are as mortal beings for Him to notice us and choose to use us in His sovereign plans.

I made my way amidst all the rocks and ice, and quickly returned to the tent where everyone was gathered, words spilling out faster than I could pronounce them.

-"Michael, Michael, He's outside! I just saw him mounted on a white horse! Come out and see what the sky looks like!"

Without a second to waste, everyone rushed outside. This night was different from all the others. Up until then, every time the Sun went down, we had always felt this constant oppression together with the glares that surfaced out of the darkness in an effort to stalk us. But this night was different; there was peace all around. The white mountains lit up by the moon, together with the millions of stars twinkling in the heavens shone in a spectacular way. It looked like there was a silver crown emerging from base camp. There was victory and redemption in the air, but that still was not the end of our story. God had warned us that he would destroy everything and the instruments of His wrath were taking their positions.

-"What and how would it happen?" was the question that caused unrest in our soul as we went to bed.

Interestingly, none of the climbers who usually came to visit stopped by that evening. All the tents were dark and the only light that could be seen came from our dining tent.

Where was everyone? And how could we warn them of the impending danger?

Judgment
and the Exodus

I went to bed meditating on everything that had happened on that supernatural day. We could still feel the fire of God to such an extent that we spent the night with our sleeping bags open because of the heat.

It was about five in the morning when I heard a very strange sound I had never heard before. Nights at base camp tended to be very noisy due to constant avalanches and rocks that would come crumbling down from above. However, they didn't pose any danger since our tents were pitched quite a distance away from those foothills. We could also here the constant cracking of ice in the glacier, like an angry screeching cat. There was even the possibility of hearing a Yeti, the legend of the abominable snowman, that also comes from Everest's mountain massif, which some swear to have heard and others to have seen.

However, the sound I was hearing was different. It was more like a stampede, but different from the warhorses I had previously heard thundering in the heavens.

The noise started to get louder, so I decided to get dressed and open my tent to see if I could make out what it was. When to my surprise, I saw sixty yaks entering our camp led by their shepherds.

I hurried outside, since I didn't not what they were doing there. Who had called them? They were definitely not heading towards another campsite, since they stopped to set up at ours.

I called one of the guides over so he could help me ask the chief shepherd in Nepalese what they were doing there.

> -"You called us over, didn't you? Your men went throughout the mountains hiring yaks to bring them here early this morning," replied the chief shepherd.

I was flabbergasted. I could not believe it. I was in awe. God had mobilized his angels to bring those yaks, so nothing would be lost. There is not a single detail that escapes His hand.

Once again, my eyes shed tears of gratitude and amazement of how His love continued to surprise us time and time again.

Time was running out and we had to take the camp down, load it up and leave in less than five hours. So, I woke everyone up and got hard to work.

Some of the Sherpa leaders from the other campsites asked whether we'd be interested in selling some of our mountaineering gear when they saw us packing. We gave away many of our items and sold others at a very low price just to have some cash available for our return trip, since we had no idea what to expect from Santa Subba. We tried to warn them about the incoming danger, but they either didn't understand or didn't believe us. So, we blessed them and prayed for them.

Just a few minutes before ten, the Sherpas and yaks began making their way out of the camp with us right behind them. We weren't able to say goodbye to our friends, since they had already headed out towards the mountains. We were greatly saddened by this, seeing that we were unable to warn them of the approaching destruction. All we could do was intercede for God's protection over them.

As we left, we sang songs of worship for the victory God had given us. One could sense freedom in the atmosphere, but also judgment, just like the angels must have felt when they entered the city of Sodom and Gomorrah to destroy it.

It was about noon, we had left base camp behind and were now hiking through the moraine headed towards Gorak-Shep. Everest was covered with a transparent veil made up of ice crystals in the form of a half-moon, shaped net that looked beautiful from a distance.

Suddenly, our singing was interrupted by a loud rumbling noise, like a bomb going off, echoing through the mountain range. We turned around startled, since everything shook with the roar of the blast.

A giant avalanche was quickly descending from Everest's heights. It seemed like half of the mountain was collapsing over the Icefall and Base Camp. The vibrations were so strong that it triggered avalanches on both the Lohtse and Nuptse peaks.

The jolt was so powerful that we were left in a state of shock, weeping from a reverential fear that came upon us. Base Camp had completely disappeared. The avalanche cloud rose covering all three peaks that made up the mountain range.

We could not speak, move nor hardly breathe from the impact. Memories of our experiences and dear friends raced through our minds at dizzying speeds. They had been buried alive under tons of snow. Our inability to warn them consumed us with a painful sorrow. We could see their faces smiling, the Spanish doctor saving Greg's life, the Italian philosophers describing the mysteries of the universe while preparing espressos for us and the French with dumbfounded looks on their faces as they heard us share about God.

They had been like a family in the mountains...and now, their souls vanished as ghosts on the ice of Everest's vast graveyard.

We wept bitterly, probably feeling the same thing Lot had felt when he watched Sodom and Gomorrah abolished. He could feel the coals of fire and brimstone consuming the city behind him, as his friends and neighbors were set ablaze with incandescent fire.

We felt that same sensation, unable to move for quite a while. Even the Sherpas with us were stunned, stating that they had never seen a triple avalanche of that magnitude. "We must keep moving. We cannot stay here," stressed Jose, the Sherpa, who was leading us, with a trembling voice.

Gradually, still reflecting on what had just taken place, we began to move on. The mountains on the moraine were lit up with a cloud of fire, something quite strange for that time of day. Then suddenly, we could make out what appeared to be two white figures shining like the sun, in the midst, of that fiery blaze.

Our hope and spirits were lifted as we were filled with a supernatural peace.

Once we had arrived at Gorak Shep, we entered a teahouse to rest and replenish some of our strength. As we opened the door, we were so relieved to see the entire Spanish team there, who had left that morning for breakfast at the station. They were also just as elated to see us, believing that the avalanche had taken our lives as well. We embraced each other as if they had truly just resurrected. After all, deep inside, that's exactly how we felt.

-"What do you know about the others?" I asked anxiously, expecting to hear some good news.

-"We haven't heard anything. We didn't see anyone this morning."

Saddened by the response, we sat down to eat with them. That great avalanche was the subject of the day, since they were planning to return to Base Camp and see if they could recover any of their belongings. If they did not find anything, they would have to cancel the expedition and head back to Katmandu.

We said goodbye and headed towards the Italian research station, known as the "the Pyramid" that was on the way. They had built a luxury hotel there. And by "luxury" in high mountain contexts, I mean that there were real beds, comforters, showers and a famous restaurant known for their yak filets. That's it. With what little money we had made from selling our equipment at base camp, we were able to book a night there. A little comfort would go a long way in helping us recover our strength and spirit to go on.

Leaving the moraine and the area we normally referred to as the shadow of death, felt like coming back to life. It had been two weeks since we had last seen any sign of vegetation or animal life, except for the crows at Base Camp.

It was quite a sight to see the first few wild flowers and some patches of green grass growing in the rocks. It reminded us of who we were and where we came from. It made us aware that there was a tender and gentle world awaiting us. Sure, it might sound simple, but not seeing a single green shrub in a long time can be devastating, disconnecting us from the reality we were created for.

As we arrived at the hotel, we found out that our Italian friends had checked in after the avalanche, and they were safe. We also got word that all those from the Spanish and French expeditions were alive. The only expedition that was unaccounted for was the Korean one. There was also no word on the Sherpa cooks and porters from the other expeditions, since Base Camp was completely cut off from every form of communication.

Although, the Koreans were the only team that never shared with us, just the fact that they were a part of the group of climbers during that season, moved us deeply.

The mountain takes lives, and it is a well-known fact that everyone knows. But it's when you are facing death straight in the eye that everything looks different, and stops being just a story told in the book of John Krakaue's about the 1996 tragedy.23 It's only after feeling its cold arms trying to rip you out of this world, yet still surviving, that you begin to weigh out your values. Some of these become truly precious and stronger –the ones truly worthy, - while others turn to rubbish, never having been of any value whatsoever in life.

I had the same sobering feeling during the Earthquake of 1985 in Mexico City, when God's sovereign hand kept me alive. I spent days helping people trapped in the rubble and asking myself, "Why was I still alive, when thousands had perished?"

All of base camp was buried in tons of snow, and every expedition from the southeast ridge was cancelled.

The smell of death was in the air. God's judgments are just, and having heard his voice so clearly and distinctively to spare our lives filled us with enormous gratitude. That avalanche was not destined to kill anyone, but to destroy a structure of darkness that had billions of people under its deadly yoke. At least that part filled us with great satisfaction as it helped us come to know God in a deeper way. Seeing His hand opening every door in the process, shielding us from every adversity and overcoming every impossibility in the mission, was an unprecedented reward and inheritance for our lives.

However, despite all that, when justice is established, we as humans end up with a feeling of fragility. Especially when considering that it's only by His grace that we are kept from sin and harm, not because we are better than anyone else, but because He simply loved us, and we responded to that love.

The mountain was cursed, even for the inhabitants of Khumbu. One of the testimonies recorded in the Krakauer book is from a Sagarmathese Sherpa who understood the curse that was upon his people:

23 Into Thin Air by Jon Krakauer

"I am an orphaned Sherpa. My father died towards the end of the seventies on the icefall of Mount Khumbu, working as a carrier for an expedition. My mother died near Periche in 1970. Her heart couldn't bear the weight she was carrying on her back while working for another expedition. After both of my parents demise, my sister and I were sent to orphanages in Europe and the United States.

I have never returned to my country because I believe it is under a curse. My ancestors arrived in the Solo-Khumbu region, and there found refuge under Sagarmatha's shade, the mother goddess of the Earth. In exchange, they were to protect the goddess' sanctuary from intruders.
However, my fellow countrymen did what they were not supposed to. They facilitated access routes to foresters and violated every last member of the goddess's body, by treading her summit, squawking triumphantly and polluting and contaminating her bosom.

Some have had to sacrifice their lives...others offered up the lives of other individuals...I know that the people of this region are condemned just like those rich and arrogant intruders who think they can conquer the world.... This is why I have sworn never again to return. I do not want to be a part of the sacrilege."

This testimony is not meant to assert that the place was holy for us, but rather to highlight the deceptive hold the devil has over the people of that region, claiming the lives of those he desires.

One does not finish climbing the mountain when the summit is reached, or when one decides to turn back, because you still need to go down and leave it. In our case, we had to walk through the debris of a judgment that was executed, as well as some defeated spirits attempt to retaliate against us. Although they have lost their territory, they try to attack in their way out. (not that they can, but they try) This is part of thoroughly cleansing the land.

That evening, we decided to put all tension aside and enjoy a juicy, yak filet with delicious Italian pasta. After weeks of eating potatoes, vegetables and rotis (Tibetan bread), we looked like castaways eating for the first time. Sleeping on a warm mattress with our faces uncovered, and not having to avoid pointy rocks under our tent, was such a well-received pleasure. After moments of intense adrenaline, you reach a moment when you feel like you've deflated. The body releases all accumulated tension as it falls into a deep rest.

The Mortal Incident

with Ang Rita-Sherpa

The following morning, now well rested, we continued our exhausting six to eight hour trek to Periche.

Once we passed the filthy and damaged Lobuje camp, we stopped to eat at a rest area along the way.

Our guide who had gone in first, all of a sudden turned around to tell me that Ang Rita, the guide hired by Santa Subba to take us to the summit but who had cancelled, was inside. He was one of the most sought-after Sherpa guides, since he had summited Everest 13 times. I knew that his decision to draw away from our expedition was part of God's divine design, even if it had been provoked by Santa Subba's wrongful attitude.

As we walked inside, we were introduced, but before greeting us, he apologized for not being a part of our expedition.

-"Don't worry, Mr. Rita, everything is well," I replied with a smile.

He then reached out to shake my hand. The moment he touched me, he knew who I was in the spirit. His gaze turned dark and a horrendous, demonic presence emerged from his eyes. This man was Sagarmatha, the dark goddess' extension in the flesh, who had been banished and left wandering.

An extremely painful force came out of his hand. I felt like my blood circulation had stopped, and my arm was frozen for a few seconds. He smiled, faking a warm greeting, but that was far from what he was actually doing. The pain passed onto my back, as if dozens of ice daggers pierced through me.

I let go of his hand and challenged his defiant look while telling our group to leave. I could barely walk as we left. I fell to the ground, limp and ringed by the tormenting pain that had just stabbed my entire body. Everything was spinning, and I felt like I was about to lose consciousness. The white, cloudy landscape began to blur, and my soul slowly began to leave my body.

The voices of the team praying for me began to sound distant, finally becoming an indistinguishable echo.

-"Spirits of death and witchcraft, let go of her in Jesus' name!" yelled some, while others laid their hands upon me.

At that point, I passed out.

I'm not sure how much time went by, when I started hearing their desperate voices again and felt someone tapping my face to wake me up. I slowly came back, and got up but lacked the strength to walk.

Tato and Lencho almost had to drag me, as I leaned on their shoulders like crutches to continue. We had to pass through the graveyard of fallen climbers and Sherpas on our way to Periche. If going through there uphill had been a challenge, on the return, I wasn't sure if I was going to make it.

Liliana, Veronica and Michael went ahead, calling down angels to prepare a safeguarded path to cross the graveyard. They interceded with all their strength until the unmistakable presence of God's hosts started to be felt.

We passed through there as quickly as possible, voices seeming to emanate from the tombs demanding justice for the lives that were lost. It was a truly terrifying and agonizing section of the route. My weakened heart seemed to explode within me.

We finally reached the Periche lodge. They laid me down on a wooden board with cushions in one of the rooms. They helped me hydrate and the cooks prepared a cup of yak butter tea (made from Tibetan herbs, butter and milk from female yaks) to warm me up and energize me.

This diabolic trap had taken me by surprise, but the power of God within me is greater than any attack of the enemy. And although sometimes it might feel like we hit rock bottom, the blood of Jesus will always have the higher hand.

After drinking the tea, having a good dinner and taking Communion, I began to feel much better, albeit still sore from those ice stabs that had crippled me. In fact, the pain didn't leave my face and my feet for another six months.

Seeing me in that condition became a growing experience for the rest of my team, who for a moment thought they had lost their leader.

Decision making in high mountains is critical, especially when there are other lives at stake. It is much easier to follow someone else than to pave a way. It is more carefree to follow someone else's steps, than to embrace a leadership role and bear the positive or negative consequences of our boldness, our prudence or even our errors. But only those who choose to do so will ever be able to leave a permanent mark. Only those who go from a passive state of following, to a stressful role of leading, will always move ahead in life.

This brave group of people embraced the challenge that was at hand, and took up their battle weapons, fully determined to see the victory to the end with or without me. What we had endured did not form students, but heroes of faith.

The Great Surprise

The next day, we were set to arrive in Shiangboche to reunite with everyone who was praying at the rear guard. Several of them went on ahead to the valley to receive us, joyfully waving flags and playing shofars as they saw us arrive.

They were emotionally charged moments as we shared some of the special experiences we had gone through.

We had booked a helicopter to fly us all down to Lukla in groups of three.

The first couple of teams started departing early in the morning, but by eleven am, with only three of us left, clouds started to fill the sky and the helicopter was unable to make the run and pick us up. God had shown me, that just like a ship's captain, I should always be the last one to leave any dangerous territory.

The clouds would open and immediately close, this

happened for a long time. Not only did the helicopter have to make its way towards us, but also it had to find a opening in the clouds to see clearly, head towards the mountainous canyon and fly towards Lukla. The helicopters did not have a mountain-detecting radar system, so unless the mounts are seen by the naked eye, they would inevitably crash.

The cold was bone wrenching, and we were reaching our limit. Under no circumstances were we to spend another night up there. We were desperate to make it to the hotel in Katmandu, just like castaways longing to find land. The clouds continued to close in and there was not a single Sherpa left with us. Another chopper had taken the last couple of tourists, departing in fog cover.

About two hours went by, before the sky slightly opened up again and our transport arrived. We ran to get on, but the pilot shut off the engines.

-"I'm not sure I'll be able to take you. Another helicopter just fell. It was taken down by a strong gust of wind against the mountain. We're not sure if there are any survivors."

-"Were they part of our group?" I asked terrified.

-"No, it was another group of climbers they picked up at the end," he answered and added dismayed, "I told the pilot to wait, but he refused."

We felt utterly shocked and dismayed from the news and the hopelessness of our inability to leave the area.

We went up to the small airport. At least it had a smelly, yak-excrement-burning stove to warm up. We were able to drink some tea or hot chocolate while our destiny was determined.

There was finally an opening in the sky and the pilot yelled,

-"Hurry! We've got to leave now!"

We quickly climbed unto the helicopter and prayed that the clouds would not turn on us. There was a clear tunnel visible towards the narrow valley which would surely close up. We flew downward like a warplane, and felt our stomachs rise into our mouths like a sharp roller coaster drop. The flight finally stabilized, and we were able to see the beautiful river. The landscape started turning green with the dense forests below. We could see the yaks with their shepherds, along with foreign climbers rhythmically walking through the trails, which just a few weeks ago had been a part of our history.

A big surprise awaited us at Lukla. A great part of the town had come out to welcome us, assembled like a multitude, and awaiting for us to say something. They did not move, as if benumbed with faces full of expectation.

They were aware that we were returning from an expedition, because if we were about to start one, it would make sense, since Sherpas come to be hired. But a gathering like this never happens at the end of an expedition.

A few moments went by and still no one moved. We decided to improvise a skit of the story of the prodigal son and share the gospel with them. As a matter of fact, this was the entire goal of the mission: for those who had never heard of Jesus to come to know Him.

After our skit, Jose, our mountain guide, served as interpreter. We spoke to them about the love of Christ, His healing power and the salvation He had purchased for us on the cross. We then made a call for repentance of sins and to accept Jesus in their hearts. Many of them suffered from head problems due to the high altitude, or back problems due to the heavy loads they had to carry. But God began to heal them all. It was incredible; one by one, they each received Jesus in their heart. They even went out to call those that had remained in their homes, yelling that they were whole and to come to know Jesus. They rushed in hoards, and received Him as their Lord and Savior. There was hardly anyone we did not pray for.

God was giving us the entire town of Lukla, as the first spoils of this extraordinary intercessory initiative. Our hearts overflowed with joy.

Not One Hair Falls Without His Will

We arrived at the Everest Hotel in Katmandu and sorted through the enormous amount of canvas luggage that was to be put away in our rooms and the storehouse, when suddenly a loud uproar burst into the hotel lobby.

Paramedics, climbers and a man on a stretcher rushed in. They communicated over their radios and made arrangements with the airport for an emergency evacuation. Everyone was speaking at the same time and no one understood what was happening.

We finally found out that it was the leader of a Columbian expedition who was climbing Everest on the North Face, when his hernia ruptured. According to reports, it was also an expedition of a spiritual nature. However, in their case, they were seeking to take Thor's hammer to the summit of the world.

When Liliana heard that the man was one of her fellow countrymen, although he was from the enemy's camp, she rushed over with great mercy to share the gospel with him. The man greatly touched and in great pain, repented of his audacious endeavor, asking God for forgiveness and receiving Jesus in his heart.
Interestingly though, as we further inquired, they explained that his hernia had ruptured on September 22nd around noon. The exact day we had planted God's flag on the mountain. That was the day God judged the Great Babylon.

Furthermore, the avalanche that buried base camp the following day caused all expeditions that Fall to be cancelled.[24] The only flag that was placed that year to consecrate Everest was the one that established the Father, the Son and the Holy Spirit, as the sole sovereign ruler in the heights of the Earth.

Universal law dictates that a minor king cannot be established where a major King rules. The King of kings and Lord of lords had sat down on the world's summit and no king or god would ever be able to dethrone Him.
Two years later, when I was wrestling for the spiritual liberation of Iraq and the fall of its dictator Sadam Hussein, we entered the Babylonian ruins. We were in the hall whose name was, the throne, room when the guide mentioned something that amazed both Liliana (who was with me) and I.

"Every year, a grand feast is held in this hall to celebrate the Day of Babylon on September 22nd."

I will never cease to be amazed at how God does things with exact precision. Those who are willing to heed His voice and obey are led through pre-established steps with uncanny accuracy.

Do you recall how I mentioned the importance of the number 22 in a previous chapter? We spoke about it when Edmund Hillary's wife and daughter died 22 years after his climb and how we climbed 22 years later. This time, Babylon was judged on that same day since its celebration is on the 22nd. It was also on a 22nd day that we conquered the Popocatepetl Volcano. And finally it was also the day that God called us to climb Everest.

Ana & Lencho climbing the Icefall on September 22nd.

Held Hostage in Katmandú

It was now time to bid farewell to Doris and her group, as well as Rony and the rest of the Latin-American team. Only four intercessors were left: Tato, Lencho, Vero and I. That afternoon, Santa Subba who had been nowhere in sight up to then, showed up at the hotel with a very wrong attitude.

-"I will not be returning your passports until you pay every last cent you owe me," he arrogantly and contemptuously threatened seeking to intimidate us.

-"That's abduction! Exclaimed Tato very upset. "We will call the police right now!"

I tried to calm him down and asked him to let me deal with the situation.

"First of all, I think you and I have to work out some numbers, because what we received from you is not worth even half of the money we have already paid you. My friend is right. What you are doing is literally holding us hostage."

> -"Then we will see you in court and let the judge decide on your money and the passports," he said in a menacing tone, before turning around and leaving.

We looked at one another puzzled and said, "Now what are we going to do?"

> -"We will think of something, let's eat. We haven't had anything since the morning," added Lencho, with a face denoting hunger.

We were finishing up lunch when a well-dressed, Nepalese man arrived on the scene with a document in his hand.

> -"Ms. Mendez?"

> -"Yes, that's me," I replied.

He handed me the envelope and left. It was a subpoena to meet with Santa Subba and his attorney for arbitration. We had to hire an attorney in Katmandu that would defend us. The question was where and how?

There were no laptops, internet or Google back then. We didn't even have cell phones.

One of the Americans who had remained behind, in case we needed anything, decided to solve the issue of securing legal council.

Growing up in a third-world country like Mexico, one becomes familiar with the terrible levels of corruption, bribery and sold out judges. However, Katmandu was not even considered a third-world country. It was so underdeveloped, with unimaginable levels of oppression and poverty, that one could easily deem it under the standard of that category.

If people could be convinced that their gods were rats with whom they had to have communion and eat with, what kind of justice system could we possibly expect?

In the meantime, we only had enough money to cover our bare necessities such as food and lodging. We had to wait for Doris to arrive in the United States to see if she could get us some additional financial help.

The amount due would increase with each passing day and we were literally being kidnapped unable to escape. We were trusting that the same God who had spared us from so many things, would not let us down after such an amazing victory.

An Unknown Weapon

The American was able to secure an attorney that would charge us $1,500 dollars to handle the case.

-"If we don't win the case, I will cover the attorney costs myself," he kindly agreed.

-"You have already gone through so much, but I want you to allow me to fight this battle because you're not very acquainted with the weapons needed for this battle, but I am."

I felt a bit insulted. After all, We had just won one of the greatest battles of our lives, and this American was now telling me that I wasn't to well acquainted with my weapons. Anyway, I just laughed on the inside, and decided to see what he had in store.

-"Fine, I want to see how you'll beat this," I jested. He laughed, feeling confident.

-"You'll see!"

The following morning, the American and I went to meet with the attorneys and Santa Subba.

Arrogantly, Mr. Subba's attorney presented a document

stating that he would return our passports if we paid him $50,000 dollars.

My partner took the document with a serious attitude and unexpectantly broke into a roaring laughter that he ended up passing it unto me. In the midst of the laughter, he returned the document, barely able to articulate that there was no way we would accept the terms.

Subba talked with his associates and not quite understanding what was happening while looking at us like we were half-mad, reconsidered their demand.

We had almost gained our composure, when they changed their offer, this time asking for $40,000 dollars instead. The American took it, analyzed it once again and began to laugh uncontrollably, rubbing it off on me as I started to laugh as well, and returned the document.

The same thing happened over and over until the amount was down to $10,000 dollars. The whole intimidation plan was brought asunder by God, shattering it with this uncontrollable and incoherent laughter that emerged from our spirit.

Since Santa Subba was getting nowhere, he got up from his seat and humbly approached me with his head down and what he said afterwards totally baffled me.

  -"Please forgive me. You are very honorable people

and I don't know why I wanted to take advantage of you."

I was shocked. The same pleasant and friendly Santa Subba I had first met had resurfaced once again. I forgave him with all my heart. I knew that in a battle of this magnitude, he had simply been a puppet in the hands of the enemy to thwart the expedition.

He then turned around and spoke to his people in a soft, quiet voice.

-"It is my client's will to give you back $10,000. He feels he has been overpaid and that this is fair. Please receive it with his most sincere apologies."

We embraced as friends and blessed Nepal and all its people.

There are weapons that go far beyond any possible reasoning. Laughter, in the midst of intimidation, was one of them. Indeed, I have used it many times to overcome several battles and difficult circumstances.

-"That blessed American finally knew a weapon I was not familiar with!"

In essence, using an opposite spirit is the key to winning battles. It is about defeating evil with good, blessing those who hurt us and speak evil against us, loving our enemies and doing unto others as we would have them do unto us. These are after all the Master's golden rules.

It is only with a spirit filled with the love of God that we can overcome every adversity and win every battle. Love is the light that cast out all darkness and the essence of the Gospel.

The Fruit

Our names were not recorded on the official Nepalese records, but they are recorded in heaven, throughout each and every place we trekked on that mountain range, and in the history of all things that have taken place as a result of that conquest.

Since 1998, the Christian population in Nepal, according to official records, grew from approximately 500 people to well over 560,000. The believers in that area stated that they have increased to up near two million believers around the year 2010. Nepal is currently the country with the greatest rate of Christian growth in the 10/40 window. There is now a beautiful church that serves the inhabitants of Lukla. There had never been one before.

Justin Long, one of the editors at Charisma magazine, and associate of the World Christian Encyclopedia, explains: "What is most remarkable is that Christianity is growing rapidly in places where just a few decades ago were considered unreachable." The Aid to the Church in Need (AED) 2004 report states that there are 576,000 Christians in the Himalayan Kingdom (only 7,000 Catholics).

A protestant missionary calculated that there were 25 Christians in Nepal in 1960. Justin Long now states that there are over 1 million Christians.[25]

India opened up around 1998, allowing the broadcasting of Christian programming for the first time ever. According to statistics by several great Evangelists of our time, they began to celebrate great crusades in that country from that date forward. It is estimated that there are approximately 90 million Christians today, the majority in the northern part of India and the adjacent regions of Nepal and Bhutan.

The first church in Bhutan opened in 1998.

A Bible printing press was established in China after so many years of missionaries having to sneak Bibles in. We found out about this through the testimony of the End-Time Handmaidens and Servants International ministry led by Gwen Shaw.

On the western side of the Himalayas, many Muslim Imams began having visions of Jesus Christ, even during the Ramadan celebration.

Our ministry has collaborated with several missions

25) http://www.fluvium.org/textos/iglesia/igl411.htm

helping to train hundreds of pastors in Tibet, Burma, Thailand, Cambodia and Vietnam. The gospel grew tremendously in these countries from 1998 forward.

The 10/40 window is no longer a closed area where the Gospel of Christ is prohibited. Today, millions of people have come to know the Light of Christ in this region of the Earth.

This is the work of God who united His Church in over 140 countries to intercede for this dark part of the globe permeating the layers of darkness that held it captive.

Over 70 million intercessors and a small group of inexperienced climbers, bold in God, who believed they could achieve the impossible, put their faith into action.

Through God we will do valiantly,
for it is He who shall tread down our enemies!
Psalms 60:12

To God the Father, to Jesus Christ and the Holy Spirit be all the Glory, who has given us the victory.

There is still much more that needs to be done and God needs bold and courageous people. He needs men and women with true conviction of faith, the true sons and daughters of God who will take His Truth throughout the whole Earth.

THE END

If you enjoyed reading this book, we recommend you watch the documentary video by Dr. Ana Méndez Ferrell

Operation Ice Castle: Mount Everest Expedition

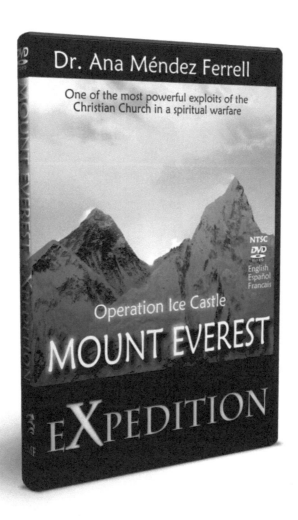

Get trained with our video courses

On Demand

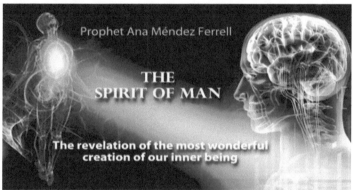

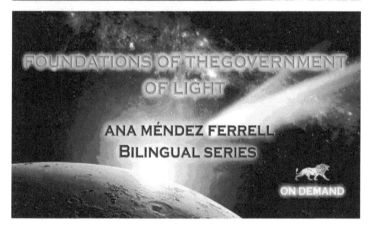

Watch us on **Frequencies of Glory TV** and **YouTube**
Follow us on **Facebook**, **Instagram** and **Twitter**

www.frequenciesofglorytv.com
www.youtube.com/user/VoiceoftheLight

https://m.facebook.com/AnaMendezFerrellPaginaOficial
www.instagram.com/anamendezferrell
www.twitter.com/AnaMendezF

Contact us today!

Voice of The Light Ministries
P.O. Box 3418
Ponte Vedra, FL. 32004
USA
904-834-2447

www.voiceofthelight.com

Made in United States
Troutdale, OR
12/14/2023

15864385R00166